Simple & Delicious
MAKE-AHEAD AND FREEZE RECIPES

Quarto.com

© 2024 Quarto Publishing Group USA Inc.
Text © 2012, 2018 Jessica Getskow Fisher

First Published in 2024 by New Shoe Press, an imprint of The Quarto Group,
100 Cummings Center, Suite 265-D, Beverly, MA 01915, USA.
T (978) 282-9590 F (978) 283-2742

Essential, In-Demand Topics, Four-Color Design, Affordable Price
New Shoe Press publishes affordable, beautifully designed books covering evergreen, in-demand subjects. With a goal to inform and inspire readers' everyday hobbies, from cooking and gardening to wellness and health to art and crafts, New Shoe titles offer the ultimate library of purposeful, how-to guidance aimed at meeting the unique needs of each reader. Reimagined and redesigned from Quarto's best-selling backlist, New Shoe books provide practical knowledge and opportunities for all DIY enthusiasts to enrich and enjoy their lives.

Visit Quarto.com/New-Shoe-Press for a complete listing of the New Shoe Press books.

New Shoe Press titles are also available at discount for retail, wholesale, promotional, and bulk purchase. For details, contact the Special Sales Manager by email at specialsales@quarto.com or by mail at The Quarto Group, Attn: Special Sales Manager, 100 Cummings Center, Suite 265-D, Beverly, MA 01915, USA.

10 9 8 7 6 5 4 3 2 1

ISBN: 978-0-7603-9102-0
eISBN: 978-0-7603-9103-7

The content in this book was previously published in *Not Your Mother's Make-Ahead and Freeze Cookbook, Revised and Expanded Edition* (The Harvard Common Press 2018) by Jessica Getskow Fisher.

Library of Congress Cataloging-in-Publication Data available

Photography: Maria Siriano

Printed in China

Simple & Delicious
MAKE-AHEAD AND FREEZE RECIPES

····································

JESSICA FISHER

····································

NEW SHOE PRESS

Contents

Introduction

This is *Not* Your Mother's Make-Ahead and Freeze Cookbook

Dinnertime. The word can evoke memories of lively voices, cozy suppers, and candlelight; images of forks chasing the last morsels of this or that on the plate; flavors blending in a happy symphony; satisfied hearts and tummies—contentment.

But the notion of dinnertime can also bring to mind that frantic feeling of coming home tired, and the dog is barking, the phone is ringing, and the entire household is clamoring, "What's for dinner?"

You grope for an answer. Fast food? TV dinners? Canned soup? These are all quick fixes, but at what cost? All have excess sodium and additives, dubiously sourced ingredients, and questionable taste. What can you do to make mealtimes more enjoyable without resorting to less-than-best menu options? How can you make contentment, not stress, the norm at dinnertime?

Turn to your freezer—what Alton Brown calls "the most potent food-preservation device ever devised." That precious appliance can save your bacon when it comes to putting healthy, wholesome meals on the table in record time.

I've been preparing make-ahead and freeze meals for over twenty years now, since I was a young high-school teacher with no one to feed but my husband and myself. Today I cook for a small army of eight: me, my husband, and our six children, of every age and size. While I have my fair share of "Calgon, take me away" moments, mealtimes are usually pleasurable at our house. I have my freezer to thank for that.

Good eating has always been part of our family culture, from enjoying upscale Santa Barbara restaurants during our dating years to laughing as our first-born, at ten months, devoured peach salsa from a spoon to grilling pizzas today on the backyard barbecue for a pack of famished children. For us, mealtimes are an event.

And while I love to cook, as a work-at-home mom, I also like to enjoy time with my family. Or by myself! Making many meals ahead of time allows me to have the best of all worlds, including some time to put my feet up. I regularly spend focused time in the kitchen, cooking up a storm and stashing the results away in the freezer for later use. The outcome? Perfect homemade convenience foods that serve us well, without undue stress.

In as little as an hour a week, you, too, can stock your freezer with make-ahead meals and meal components that are tasty, filling, healthy, and budget-friendly.

But don't worry: These are not your mother's—or your grandmother's—frozen casseroles. Drawing on modern technology and a global food market full of diverse ingredients, the recipes that follow feature a wide variety of flavor profiles and cooking methods. They appeal to modern taste buds, and they can all be prepared in bulk to help you save time in the kitchen. These meals will put the lively conversation and cozy suppers back into your dinnertimes.

The Case for Make-Ahead and Freeze Meals

Home cooks lead busy lives. Students, single parents, stay-at-home moms, work-at-home parents, working professionals, retired folks—all are looking for delicious meals that are easy and affordable. They crave tasty meals, but due to lack of planning, lack of knowledge, or simply a lack of cooking mojo, they settle for less than the best. Deep down, lots of folks feel there must be a better and easier way to eat well. Many of our mothers practiced cook-and-freeze methods. Whether they engaged in a once-a-month marathon kitchen session or spent a harvest season preserving the surplus vegetables and fruits on hand, the cooks who came before us were known to stash meals and meal components away in the deep freeze.

Unfortunately, many of those dishes were forgotten in deep storage and developed a serious case of frostbite. Or, worse, they weren't all that tasty to begin with. If you remember the heavy, starch-laden casseroles of yesteryear, you might think you want to pass on homemade frozen entrées.

But times, technology, and tastes have all changed. And a freezer packed with ready-to-go breakfasts, lunches, and dinners can be a boon to any home cook. Taking a different approach to food preparation and storage could change your kitchen, your mealtimes, and your life.

Many of today's home cooks either are intimidated by the prospect of cooking many meals at once or simply don't know where to start in freezing foods for later enjoyment. Some have never even heard of "freezer cooking." Others may enjoy cooking but lack the time and energy to spend hours in the kitchen, especially after a full day of work.

But freezer cooking can provide a handy solution to dinner dilemmas. Imagine enjoying inexpensive, healthy, tasty meals any night of the week. Picture your freezer stocked with several weeks' worth of easy, versatile dinners that please any palate, young or old. Consider preparing a multitude of meals in just a few hours without breaking a sweat. Or the bank.

I started my cook-and-freeze adventure the traditional way, spending 8 to 24 hours shopping, chopping, and hopping about my kitchen, trying to get 30 meals ready to freeze at once. Twenty-one years ago, I was in the final stages of pregnancy, awaiting my first child and preparing to quit my job as a high-school teacher. My friend Jessika and I had read *Once a Month Cooking*, the grandmother of all freezer cookbooks, and we decided to give it a go. My pregnant, swollen feet weren't too sure about the project, but it all seemed worth it when I ended up with forty meals stashed in the freezer for the coming month and beyond.

The practice has proved to be a winner time and again.

Over the years, as my family has grown from one little baby to six active children, I have needed the convenience of premade meals all the more. But, I'm not as spry as I once was. I've been pressed to find the time and energy it takes to cook massive amounts of food in just a day or two. I've needed to find ways to fill my freezer without spending an inordinate amount of time doing it. Typical shortcuts like canned soups and sauces can't compete with my desire to feed my family less-processed, healthier foods. I want it all.

I've sought simpler ways to fill the freezer, like doing triple-batch cooking to make three lasagnas instead of one on a weeknight and mini cooking sessions wherein I create a range of meals built around one main ingredient. I've challenged myself to find the most efficient methods for cooking ahead of time.

After years of freezer cooking the traditional way, I've realized that it can be more streamlined, that I can have home-cooked meals ready and waiting, and that I don't have to spend days in the effort to pull it off—unless I want to. Instead, I have found ways to

Quick-Start Guide

Instructions for Big-Batch Cooking

Every four to six weeks, I take time out of my schedule to prepare several meals for the freezer. It's a little gift to myself, to make dinnertime easier in the weeks ahead. I might spend an hour or two cooking on a lazy afternoon, or I might wake up with the sun on a weekend day and cook all morning. It really depends on what our household needs at any given moment and what I feel like doing that day.

The one constant is the time that it saves me throughout the month as I go to the freezer for a pan of enchiladas or pop some homemade scones into the oven in a matter of seconds. My family avoids the drive-through, and we eat exceptionally well with minimal last-minute work.

On a recent Saturday afternoon, I was sorely tempted to "run for the border"—or at least the closest taco stand. After thinking through my options, I headed for my kitchen instead. I pulled a container of taco meat and a pan of enchiladas from the freezer. While those reheated in the microwave, I chopped lettuce, shredded cheese, and laid out tubs of sour cream and salsa. Within five minutes, I had assembled a complete taco bar and fed my family a feast that certainly beat anything the local taco joint had to offer. And it was thanks to make-ahead meals in my freezer.

Some folks might thumb their noses at cook-and-freeze meals. Perhaps they've had bad experiences; maybe they're haunted by a memory or two of Mom's Mystery Meat Casserole. However, those are relics of the past! I am a self-proclaimed food snob, yet after finding and developing recipes that really work for my family, I've found bulk cooking to be a happy compromise between a busy life, a tight budget, and a desire for good, home-cooked food.

condense my cooking tasks and develop bulk cooking plans that I can pull off in about five hours, sometimes an afternoon when I putter in the kitchen, sipping wine and watching BBC miniseries with my daughters.

We live in an age of instant gratification. While hard work is still important, ours is a fast-paced society. But good home cooking still has a place in it. Through careful planning and making use of modern technologies, I'm now able to prepare 20 to 30 breakfasts, lunches, or dinners in a matter of hours.

Donna Reed, it's time to meet Jane Jetson. While we may not have home vending machines producing food to order the way the Jetsons did, we can have tasty, healthy meals at the ready without an inordinate amount of work.

Efficient freezer cooking is the wave of the future—and it's definitely not your mother's frozen dinner.

Perhaps you've heard or read about this freezer-cooking thing. That it's a bit overwhelming, and you just don't have the time to figure it all out. It sounds complicated; it involves lots of charts; it takes too much time. Or maybe you're just so eager to get started that you don't want to spend time reading.

It's easier than you think! Big-batch cooking is as simple as preparing a double batch of tonight's dinner and freezing half for another night. It only takes a few minutes longer to make that second helping, but the rewards are huge: There's no extra cleanup or prep work when you serve that meal in a few weeks' time!

If you want to put away 8 to 12 meals at one time, here's a quick-start guide to cooking, freezing, and enjoying homemade meals in the weeks ahead.

1. Draw up a three-column chart to plan your big-batch cooking. Label the first column "Main Ingredient/Protein," the second column "Recipe," and the third column "Groceries."

2. Choose one protein, such as chicken, to cook for this round. Write that in the first square under "Main Ingredient/Protein." (Next time, you can make different kinds of dishes, but we're doing baby steps here.)

3. List your four favorite chicken recipes in the next column. Check out the chicken chapter, which starts on page 42, for inspiration.

4. Create a grocery list in column three based on the recipes you chose. You're going to prepare double or triple batches of each of these items, so adjust your grocery list accordingly. Check your pantry to see what you have and what you will need to buy.

5. Go shopping. Before you leave, make sure there's enough room in the fridge to store all the perishables. Do a quick clean-out if needed.

6. Prior to your freezer-cooking session, prep all your vegetables and any other ingredients that might need chopping, slicing, and dicing.

7. Let the freezer cooking begin! Prepare each recipe in assembly-line fashion. Don't forget that you're doubling or tripling recipes. For each of the four recipes, lay out two or three baking dishes to fill and put them together quickly and efficiently. Then continue with the next recipe.

8. Wrap, label, and freeze as you go. Make sure that food cools to room temperature before freezing. To enable quicker freezing and a better result, completely chill the food in the refrigerator before placing it in the freezer.

9. By the time you're done, you should have 8 to 12 dinners ready to go for the coming weeks. If you choose four simple recipes, you'll be done in a few hours. And you'll be amazed at how much time you just bought yourself.

The Basics of Freezer Cooking

When convenience-food items and home refrigeration units started to come on the scene in the first part of the twentieth century, they offered a welcome respite from all the hard work it took to put food on the table. Home cooks have always welcomed convenience, from store-bought sliced bread (1920s) to a complete frozen entrée (1940s). We are no different from our predecessors in wanting shortcuts to get us to dinnertime faster and more economically. However, modern-day convenience items are no longer "the best thing since sliced bread." They can take a huge bite out of one's budget, and they usually aren't the healthiest food choices around.

There is a better way.

Make your favorite foods ahead of time to store in the freezer for the perfect, customized convenience meals. Not only will you save time and money by cooking in bulk, you'll also be able to feed your family exactly what you want to feed them instead of settling for second best.

Chill Out: What Can You Freeze?

The short answer: a lot. The variety of foods that can be partially or completely prepped ahead of time is vast. Many of your favorite meals or meal components can be made weeks in advance and stored in the freezer, enabling you to have the home-cooked meals you crave any night of the week. You will be surprised at the choices available to you.

Just be sure to chill all items in the refrigerator prior to stashing them in the freezer. This will help them freeze quickly and avoid freezer burn.

Complete Main Dishes

- **Meatloaf.** I like to mix and form the loaf, and then wrap and freeze it prior to baking. It tastes fresher than a loaf that's been cooked and then frozen.

- **Meatballs.** Use the same meat mix you use for meatloaves. Form the balls, bake them in the oven, and then freeze family size portions in freezer bags. Later you can turn them into simple spaghetti and meatballs with Easy Slow Cooker Red Sauce (page 89) or try the variations such as Swedish Meatballs with Dill (page 32), Barbecue Sauce for Meatballs (page 37), and *Boules de Picolat* (page 38).

- **Hamburger patties.** Quick-freeze the uncooked patties on a baking sheet lined with plastic wrap. Once the patties are frozen, place them in a freezer bag. When you're ready to serve

them, the burgers can be placed on the grill without thawing, making for quick cookouts. Alternatively, bundle the patties in dinner-size packs, separating each one by a bit of deli waxed paper and wrapping the entire bundle securely in plastic wrap.

- **Marinated meat and poultry.** Place the uncooked meats along with the marinade in a freezer bag or freezer-safe container. Freeze the marinade and meat. The meat will marinate as it thaws later in the refrigerator. Cook as you normally would.

- **Casseroles, lasagnas, and enchiladas.** Assemble several pans at once to freeze for later baking.

- **Burritos.** Prepare the burritos and seal them in freezer bags. Thaw and heat them in the microwave or crisp them on a stovetop griddle. Burritos can also be heated directly from the freezer; no need to thaw.

- **Tamales.** Leave the steamed tamales in their cornhusk wrappings. Seal them in a freezer bag. Resteam them right before serving (no need to thaw).

- **Taquitos.** Quick-freeze assembled taquitos on baking sheets, and then seal them in a freezer bag. When ready to serve, bake them without thawing.

- **Stews, soups, and chili.** Freeze these dishes in freezer-safe containers. Consider freezing individual portions in small containers for quick lunches and snacks.

Meal Components and Basic Ingredients

Meal components are simply parts of meals that are precooked or premixed in order to help you get a head start on dinner. Precooking and freezing a few meal components can save you valuable minutes in the kitchen. Seasoned ground beef, tomato sauce, marinades, sliced meats for stir-fries, cooked proteins to add to salads and sandwiches, compound butters, baking mixes, and spice blends are all homemade convenience items that you can prepare in bulk and store in the freezer for later use.

- **Seasoned ground beef.** Cool the cooked meat and store in a freezer bag or freezer-safe container. Incorporate this later into tacos, chili, casseroles, nachos, burritos, and more.

- **Meat and chicken precut for stir-fries.** Trim and slice the meat and seal it in a freezer bag or freezer-safe container, with or without a marinade. Thaw in the refrigerator before using in your favorite recipes.

- **Cooked chicken.** Cook chicken in the slow cooker or oven or poach it on the stovetop (pages 43 and 44). Chop or shred the cooked chicken and seal it in a freezer bag to use later in chicken salads, soft tacos, burritos, Asian dishes, soups, sandwich fillings, and more.

- **Carnitas and shredded beef or pork.** Place cooked meat in freezer bags or freezer-safe containers. Use it in tacos, burritos, nachos, soups, and barbecue sandwiches.

- **Pasta sauce.** Cook up a big batch of sauce, with or without meat, and store it in whatever size freezer-safe containers you like.

- **Cooked beans.** Prepare a big batch of dried beans and store them in 2-cup portions in freezer bags or freezer-safe containers. Canned beans are cheap, but home-cooked beans are cheaper!

- **Pizza dough, sauce, and toppings.** As soon as you've allowed the dough to rise for a short time, seal the dough ball(s) in freezer bags and freeze. The pizza sauce and toppings can be packaged in freezer bags or freezer-safe containers. Put together a kit so you can pull just one package out of the freezer when you're planning pizza for dinner.

- **Club warehouse purchases.** Bulk packs of cheeses, meats, and breads can be repackaged for storage in the freezer, helping you make the most of your bulk savings. Shredded cheeses like mozzarella, Cheddar, Monterey Jack, and Parmesan freeze well, as do some softer cheeses, such as goat cheese. Crumbled cheeses, including Gorgonzola, blue, and feta, also hold up well when frozen.

NOTE:

Block cheese will crumble after freezing, making it difficult to slice. Shred cheese in advance of freezing if you buy the block variety.

- **Surplus produce.** If you belong to a produce co-op or CSA, you may find yourself inundated with fresh produce at times. While enjoying it fresh from the farm is divine, letting it go to waste because you can't eat it fast enough is not. Diced or sliced bell peppers and onions, berries, and chopped or whole bananas can all be frozen without much extra preparation; freeze them on trays so that they won't stick together and then seal them in freezer bags. Other vegetables, like green beans and snap peas, can easily be blanched, cooled, and frozen for later use.

- **Dinner kits.** Grocery stores sell meal kits, packages of ingredients to put together before serving. Why not make your own? Consider preparing "dinner kits" for easy-to-assemble meals such as tacos, sloppy joes, burritos, or pizza. Cook and season meat or beans. Steam a pot of rice. Portion out the cheese. Package each of these components in meal-size portions and place all the bags for a certain meal in one larger bag. Label the bag and freeze it for later use. Transfer the bag to the refrigerator the day before serving, and the work is practically done for you come dinnertime.

- **Baking mixes and other baked goods.** If you love to bake but find yourself pressed for time, assemble your own baking mixes. When you have your dry ingredients already measured and mixed, pancakes, muffins, waffles, biscuits, brownies, and quick breads can be ready in a flash. Preformed frozen scones and biscuits bake quickly, making for a delicious morning treat. Whole-Grain Cinnamon Rolls (page 136) can be pulled from the freezer to thaw in the refrigerator overnight, providing you with freshly baked bread for breakfast or brunch the next day.

What Can't You Freeze?

There are a few things that are better left unfrozen. Here's my short list:

- **White potatoes.** Don't think you can chop up a bunch of uncooked potatoes and freeze them for later use. They generally discolor and lose texture. The best way to freeze white potatoes successfully is to cook them first.

- **Recipes containing mayonnaise.** This category includes dips, chicken salads, casseroles with mayo, and so on. The mayonnaise tends to separate, and the texture and flavor of the dish suffer.

- **Lettuce, greens, and other vegetables to use raw.** Lettuce and other salad greens should not be frozen. Most other vegetables can be frozen if they are to be cooked later, but otherwise, it's Sog City, baby.

- **Block cheeses and sliced cheeses.** These do not generally freeze well—they crumble upon defrosting—but shredded cheese can be frozen successfully. Very soft cheeses like Brie and Camembert should not be frozen.

Frozen Assets: Approaches to Freezer Cooking

In the 1990s, once-a-month cooking hit the scene. It is a method of cooking 30 meals in a day or two and freezing them for later use. And it works! I started using this technique years ago and have found it to be a great way to save time, money, and brain power. I save time when I use the assembly-line method; I save money by buying and cooking in bulk; and I save brain power by not having to think too much about what's for dinner. I can go to the freezer and grab a pan of enchiladas or a bag of taquitos for a quick dinner, thereby avoiding the fast-food trap.

Today there are a myriad of ways to approach make-and-freeze cooking in addition to the all-day cooking party:

Double (or Triple) Duty

This is perhaps the easiest and most painless way to fill your freezer. Simply double or triple tonight's dinner and freeze the extra. Do this for several nights, and your freezer will be stocked with a variety of meals. All the recipes in this book can be easily doubled or tripled, making it simple to create a freezer stash quickly.

This is my favorite strategy during busy seasons.

Short but Sweet

Mini sessions are short cooking sessions focused on preparing several meals around a certain protein or key ingredient. You might do this once a week or do several mini sessions over the course of several days. Either way, over time you will have built a massive stockpile of meals in your freezer. Grab an hour or two and do some assembly-line cooking!

Cook for a Month

In the early days of freezer cooking, cooks spent several days shopping, chopping, and hopping around the kitchen, cooking up a month's worth of meals, many of them casseroles. Today's lifestyles don't always afford such lengthy cooking sessions. With careful planning, however, three to five hours of efficient cooking time *can* result in a month's worth of meals and meal components without a lot of fuss.

Make a Day of It

While you know I favor short and sweet cooking sessions, rest easy; there's no rule that says you can't spend a day in the kitchen if you'd like to! The method you choose depends on your inclination and the time you have available. There's no "right" way to do it, except the way that works for YOU this month.

You can build your own plan, or if you're someone who just wants to get cooking, consult the Quick-Start Guide (page 8) and get to work.

Keep Your Cool: Proper Freezing Techniques

Freezing preserves food because it inhibits the action of microorganisms that would otherwise lead to spoilage. Food stored in the freezer shouldn't go "bad," as the enzyme action is effectively halted while the food is frozen. As long as you start with fresh food in the first place and the food stays frozen for the entire storage time, you shouldn't have to worry about spoilage of frozen foods. In fact, the USDA says that "frozen foods remain safe indefinitely," provided they are stored at 0°F (–18°C). However, taste and texture can be adversely affected depending on how a food is packaged and frozen and how long it is kept in cold storage.

Additionally, it can be difficult to keep a home freezer at a steady 0°F (–18°C) because typically the door is opened fairly frequently. It's a good idea to serve foods within a reasonable amount of time to ensure the best taste and texture. A general rule of thumb is not to store items longer than two to three months in the freezer compartment of a refrigerator or six months in a dedicated deep freezer.

Often, folks worry that their frozen foods will have a funny taste or develop unsightly ice crystals. These problems are easily prevented if food is cooled, packaged, and stored correctly. An understanding of the freezing process can help you maximize and preserve your food's quality.

The colder the food is before it hits the freezer, the faster it will freeze. Quick freezing keeps ice crystals small, leading to better quality control, less cell damage, and less loss of moisture upon thawing. Large ice crystals, formed during slow freezing, can hurt the texture of the food, causing it to lose moisture and resulting in dry, tasteless food. Therefore, chilling a dish in the refrigerator before freezing it is always a good idea.

Your goal is to have food taste as good or better on the other side of freezing. (And yes, some flavors do improve upon freezing.)

Warm food releases moisture or steam into the air. If you cover the food before it has had a chance to cool, the steam will condense on the inside of the lid. Warm food placed in the freezer will take longer to freeze, and upon freezing, it will have lots of large unsightly ice crystals.

One approach, which I recommend, is to allow hot foods to cool slightly, uncovered, at room temperature, before refrigerating them. While hot foods can be refrigerated safely, your refrigerator will have to work harder to cool them. Once a food has cooled slightly at room temperature, you can chill it thoroughly in the refrigerator before freezing it. Keep in mind that perishable food should never stand at room temperature longer than two hours.

Frozen food should stay at 0°F (−18°C) or colder. A freezer thermometer is essential to keeping your food fresh. A freezer alarm is even better. An inexpensive gadget, a freezer alarm will alert you when the freezer's temperature rises to an unsafe temperature. There is almost nothing more discouraging to a cook than finding a freezer full of food thawing and spoiling due to a power outage, blown fuse, or a freezer door inadvertently left slightly open. Installing a freezer alarm can save your bacon—and your ice cream sandwiches, too.

That's a Wrap: A Variety of Packaging Methods

There are several methods for packaging food for the freezer. What you use will depend on the storage space you have available and the foods you are preparing to freeze.

Using Zip-Top Freezer Bags

Zip-top freezer bags are great for storing meats, baked goods, and other items that hold their own shape. You can save space by putting soups, stews, or beans in these as well—but there is a possibility of leakage. Always thaw a zip-top freezer bag full of food on a tray in the refrigerator to catch any drips.

One of the benefits of zip-top bags is that they can be laid flat, frozen, and then lined up like books on a shelf or stacked like pancakes. They provide a great way to store a lot of food in a small amount of space. You can reuse bags that you've used for baked goods and baking mixes; simply store the empty bags in the freezer until next time. Never reuse bags that have held raw meat, poultry, or seafood.

When using zip-top freezer bags, be sure to remove as much air as possible from the bag before sealing it. You can easily use a straw to suck out the air from bags holding fruits, vegetables, or baked goods. Seal the bag almost completely, squeezing out as much air as you can with your hands. Then insert a plastic drinking straw into a small gap in the seal. Suck out any remaining air, pinching the bag's seal and the straw closed as the plastic encloses itself around the food. Remove the straw and seal the bag quickly to prevent air from reentering the bag. While this may seem like an odd method, it is quite effective in removing excess air from the bags. Do not use this technique with uncooked meats or seafood, to avoid contact with bacteria.

There are also commercial freezer bags with valves available, but they are rather expensive compared to the handy duo of freezer bag and drinking straw.

Quick freezing or *open freezing* is the practice of individually freezing items like scones, berries, or burgers on trays and then transferring them to freezer bags or closed containers for longer-term freezing. When foods are frozen this way, it isn't necessary to thaw the entire package to use just a few items. You can simply remove the number of items you plan to serve while leaving the rest in the freezer. Freezer bags are ideal for storing these quick-frozen items.

Using Plastic Containers with Lids

Reusable/disposable plastic containers with lids are wonderful for storing foods like sauces, soups, and stews. These are leak-proof, making them ideal at thawing time and quick for reheating. Since slightly frozen foods will pop out easily from the container into the stockpot for stovetop reheating, you won't need to wait for them to thaw completely.

This type of container doesn't last forever; the plastic tends to etch, stain, or wear down over time, but they are a nice, inexpensive option. They also lend themselves to gifting food items easily and not worrying about getting the containers back.

Using Aluminum Baking Pans

You may recognize aluminum baking pans from that frozen lasagna you bought in the freezer section that time. Caterers use disposable steam pans at buffet events. They come in a variety of sizes and strengths and are available at discount stores, food service shops, and even party stores. My favorites come in a variety of colors with aluminum lids.

Disposable aluminum baking pans are very convenient, especially if you know you'll be giving meals as gifts or taking them to potluck dinners. The brands that come with sturdy aluminum lids are the ones to buy; they make wrapping up your freezer meals especially quick and easy and add extra stability for stacking in the freezer. While disposables are not everyone's favorite, they are certainly convenient.

Using Glass or Metal Baking Dishes

Glass or metal baking dishes are the longest lasting of the freezer-friendly packaging choices. If you have a large supply, they are your best bet. If you have a limited supply, you might not want to have all your pans sitting in the freezer when you decide to bake an impromptu cake.

I keep multiples of many sizes of these pans as they are my favorite vessels to store mashed potatoes, enchiladas, and other meals that I want to pop straight into the oven. Some glass bakeware comes with plastic lids for storage, reducing the need for foil or other wrappings. These are wonderful options, as they are completely reusable and stack beautifully in the freezer.

Using Fancy Sealing Machines

Vacuum-sealing machines that encase your food in airtight plastic are also available. These are said to protect extremely well against freezer burn. I have one and loved using it that first month I got it. After that, however, it proved to be bulky to store and a pain to haul in from the garage whenever I needed it.

Additionally, these machines are costly to purchase, as are the special plastic bags they require. A vacuum sealer generally works best for food items that hold their shape, such as steaks or loaves of bread. They cannot be easily used for liquids.

Using Common Sense (a.k.a. Labeling Your Meals)

However you package your foods, be sure to label them with the date, the name of the contents, and the cooking or reheating instructions, if applicable. It's easy to forget once something's been in cold storage for a while. Some foods change color when frozen, making it difficult to determine what they are. The last thing you want to do is confuse mushroom gravy with chocolate fudge sauce.

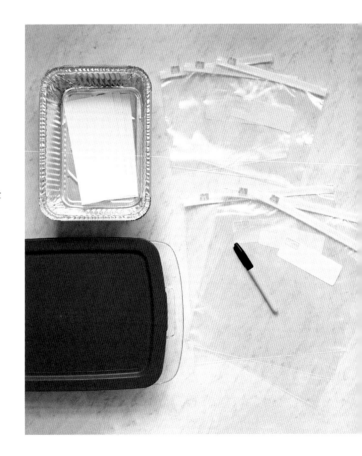

A Tight Squeeze: What About Freezer Space?

Although I do currently own a large deep freezer, that hasn't always been the case. I know from years of personal experience that you don't need a dedicated freezer to make freezer cooking work for you. In fact, when I started practicing this mode of cooking, I owned the smallest refrigerator known to man. It was only one step up from a dorm fridge, but it regularly held the makings of a dozen or more meals at a time.

Here are some suggestions for making it work with whatever freezer you have:

- Start with a mostly empty freezer. You won't be able to store several weeks' worth of meals in it if it already holds multiple containers of ice cream, loaves of bread, and packages of hamburger. Consider "eating down the freezer" prior to a big cooking session so that you can reduce what is already there. Hold off on buying a lot of other frozen foods until you know how much space you will need for homemade dinners. Remember, since you're going to be making your own convenience foods, you won't need the store-bought versions anyway.

- If you already have a stockpile of frozen meats and poultry, use them as the building blocks of your make-ahead and freeze meals. Uncooked meat can be thawed, cooked, and refrozen without loss of taste or texture. You won't need much extra space for these meals; you're simply going to take the frozen hamburger or chicken out, thaw it, cook it up, give it a makeover, and put it back where it was, transformed from a frozen raw ingredient into a homemade, frozen convenience food.

- Use freezer bags. Zip-top freezer bags, designed for cold temperatures and durability, can hold many kinds of frozen foods. These are especially useful for meats in marinades, taco fillings, pizza dough, and some thicker stews and chilis. As you cool, label, and freeze the food in these bags, seal them and lay them flat in your freezer. Once they are frozen, you will be able to stand them on end and line them up like books on a shelf, making the best use of your storage space. Make sure that you remove as much excess air as possible before sealing the bag in order to avoid freezer burn.

- Use similarly shaped plastic containers. For liquids, like pasta sauce, use containers that are all the same shape and size. These will stack well and make the best use of your space. Square containers fill space more efficiently than round ones.

- Organize like with like. If you have three 9 × 13-inch (23 × 33 cm) pans, stack those on top of each other. Stash all your sauce containers in one spot. Line up all your freezer bags like books on a shelf. Not only will those meals be easier to find, you'll also make the most of your space.

- Consider freezing meal components. Casseroles are big and bulky. Your average refrigerator-freezer can only hold so much, but if you use meal components as a preferred dinnertime shortcut, you can make the most of it, stashing a vast quantity of meats, vegetables, grains, and other building blocks in a small amount of space.

GOOD LABELING

Accurate labeling is key to enjoying your frozen meals to the fullest. Be sure to include the following:

1. Date, so that you can eat the food within 2 to 3 months, ideally.

2. Recipe name: no mystery meat!

3. Baking/serving instructions, so that you don't have to hunt down the recipe in order to figure out how to serve the meal.

Breaking the Ice: Proper Thawing

What about thawing? Some foods, like unbaked pies, don't need to be thawed prior to baking and serving. Soups and chilis can be thawed and reheated in a pot on the stove. Frozen burritos can be baked or microwaved directly from the freezer.

But other foods, like lasagna, meats, and casseroles, do best when completely defrosted prior to cooking. This should be done in the refrigerator, not on the counter, so that the thawing food does not reach unsafe temperatures. Place zip-top freezer bags and foil-wrapped packages on a tray to catch drips before stowing them in the refrigerator. A slow thaw also allows the food to reabsorb some of the moisture it lost when it was frozen.

You'll have a better-tasting meal if it's had adequate time to thaw, so plan ahead and pull out two or three meals at a time to defrost in the refrigerator. Some will thaw more quickly than others. If you have a variety of items thawing in the refrigerator, you'll have some options come dinnertime.

Cash for Your Cache: Freezer Cooking Can Save You Money

One of the most tangible benefits of freezer cooking is that it can save you money. Here's how:

- **You can buy in bulk.** Ever shake your head in wonder at folks who shop at warehouse clubs and come home with ginormous packages of food? Large families like mine go quickly through a bulk pack of chicken breasts or a 5-pound (2270 g) bag of shredded cheese, items that can often be a terrific bargain. But smaller households may have a harder time using up those huge packages. With freezer cooking, you can easily reap the cost savings from that bulk package. Divide a 5-pound (2270 g) bag of cheese into smaller meal-size bags for tacos, burritos, or pizzas. Divvy up the bulk pack of chicken breasts into zip-top freezer bags, add a marinade to each bag for good measure, and you're halfway to dinnertime.

- **You can avoid processed foods.** Processed foods have one major thing going for them—convenience. They help us save time and get us from hungry to fed in short order. But there's a cost involved, and processed foods aren't always the best tasting or healthiest choices. By putting a few hours of work into cooking and freezing foods prepared from scratch, you can avoid the junk.

- **You can limit your takeout.** Although I love to have someone else do the cooking, I know that eating too many restaurant meals isn't good for our health or our pocketbooks. Having a stash of freezer meals on hand helps us avoid takeout and keeps some extra cash in our pockets.

- **You can go grocery shopping less often.** Since I do big shopping trips to do big cooking, I go grocery shopping less frequently. Frequent shopping can lead to impulse buys, so staying out of the store saves me money by helping me avoid those unnecessary purchases.

How to Swing the Deal

Although your overall monthly grocery bill will probably be lower when you switch to freezer cooking, it can initially be difficult to fund a bulk cooking session. I currently feed my family of eight on less than $1,300/month, the amount the USDA allots as "frugal" for a group of our size, sex, and ages, in part because I practice big-batch cooking and making good use of my deep freezer. However, if I'm cooking in bulk, I'm also paying in bulk. That one grocery bill for a month's worth of meals can seem daunting. There are several ways that you can swing economical batch cooking, even on a fixed budget.

- **Use what you have on hand.** Don't make recipes that call for ingredients that might not fit your budget during this pay period. Instead, scan your fridge, freezer, and pantry for what's already on the shelves and build your menu plan from there.

- **Compare prices at different stores.** Keep track of the prices on things that you buy on a regular basis and note which stores have the best prices. You may be surprised that there's a vast price difference between Store A and Store B.

- **Practice stockpiling.** Buy ingredients you use frequently in larger quantities when they are on sale, rather than paying full price later when you need them. If you make this a regular practice, you'll find that you can keep a fuller pantry. Provided you don't buy more than you will use in a reasonable length of time, this is wise investing. If my local store has a great price on chuck roast one week, I will probably buy several packages and store them in the freezer until my next bulk cooking session. Good sale prices tend to repeat every six weeks. This kind of stockpiling works for all ingredients, except for some fresh produce items and other foods that have a short shelf life.

- **Straddle the sales.** Find out the beginning and ending dates of your local grocery stores' sales. Build your menus around the sale items from two consecutive weeks. Usually, you can get an ad for the new sale the night before it starts, sometimes sooner. Just check your junk mail or ask at your store. If you don't mind going shopping on back-to-back days, you can take advantage of two weeks' worth of sales in one week. Some stores even offer double-ad days, where they overlap the two weeks' sales for one day. Shop the week you plan to cook to maximize the ingredients' freshness.

- **Cook enough meals or meal components to last longer than one month.** If you find a great deal on a main ingredient, buy enough for two months of meals. For instance, at the beginning of one month, I can make enough Easy Slow Cooker Red Sauce (page 89) to last us six to eight weeks. With proper packaging and storage, I know it will be fresh tasting for even longer. Not only does this provide us with a little more variety in our menus for both months, it also helps me offset my costs because I cooked a sale-priced item in greater quantity.

- **Make in-season recipes.** It just makes sense to cook what is in season and on sale. Easy Stovetop Ratatouille (page 83) is ideal for the summer harvest season. Sales on boneless chicken breasts are also abundant during the summer months. November and December are ideal months to prepare turkey recipes. A few birds will make several batches of enchiladas or tamales. In winter, chuck roast is often a butcher's special; use it to make stews, chilis, and ragus.

- **Build your freezer meals to feature items that you can reliably get for a good price.** Meat can be expensive, but eggs, beans, rice, and pasta are almost always good deals. You can easily make many meals based on these ingredients. Spinach and Feta Manicotti with Lemon and Oregano (page 94) and Green Chile Rice Casserole (page 81) are not only meatless, they're also built on economical ingredients.

Meal Planning: Dinnertime and Beyond

Most home managers know that having a meal plan is key to a smoothly running household. If you know what the dinner plan is, you can avoid the fast-food drive-through on the way home from soccer practice. The kids won't be crying for something to eat while you stare dazedly into the cupboards. And you can put the lively voices and candlelight back into dinnertime.

Having a freezer stocked with homemade meals facilitates meal planning. You can scan the freezer contents at the beginning of the week and decide what to serve, working around the week's activities. But freezer meals can go beyond just dinnertime. Freezer Breakfast Smoothies (pages 112–114) are quick on-the-go snacks. Foods like Chipotle Chicken and Onion Wraps (page 61) and Cheesy Butternut Squash Soup with Herbs (page 95) are great packed into a lunch box and reheated at work or school. You can work freezer cooking into good eating all day long.

These make-ahead meals can go on vacation with you, help a friend who's just had a baby, or comfort the neighbors who've just lost a loved one. Stocking your freezer does more than just provide dinner: It can improve the quality of your life, your budget, and your friendships.

Keys to Efficiency

Efficiency in bulk cooking combines the best of all worlds. You can get home-cooked food the way you want it. You have convenience on the nights you need it. You conserve valuable resources (like money, utilities, and packaging) by buying and cooking in bulk. And you don't have to spend an inordinate amount of time stocking the freezer if you use some time-saving techniques.

Here are the keys to efficient freezer cooking:

- Cooking in bulk
- Planning your meals around common ingredients and core proteins
- Making good use of the tools and technology (that is, small appliances) at your fingertips

- Using the assembly-line method to prepare several batches of a recipe at one time

Cooking in Bulk

If you cooked thirty different meals in one day, you'd have a month's worth of dinners in the freezer, but you would not have saved any time and you would be utterly exhausted. Efficient freezer cooking relies on cooking in bulk and making several "copies" of the same thing. It won't save you time unless you prepare double or triple batches of the recipes you've chosen.

You may be concerned that you will get bored with your meal choices over the month's time. But if you surveyed your eating habits over the past month, you'd probably find that you had several meals more than once during that period. People do that.

And if you include meal components in your cooking plan, you'll find that a few variations can really change up your suppers. A double batch of seasoned taco meat can go into tacos one night and fill Mexican-style omelets another night. That double batch doesn't seem so boring after all, does it? You can mix and match meal components to create a huge variety of meals.

Common Ingredients

One of the best ways to save time during a bulk cooking session is to combine common ingredients in different ways. The humble chicken breast can be transformed into Tandoori Chicken (page 48) and Creamy Chicken Enchiladas (page 59). All two meals vary in flavor, but they come from the same starting point.

Using common ingredients can also help you take advantage of grocery-store sales. If you find ground beef or steaks on special, then stock up, prepare those items in different ways, and stash the meals in the freezer for later. You'll eat well for a few bucks instead of having to pay full price when you have a hankering for a certain food—when it's not on sale.

Tools to Help You

Efficiency is the goal in freezer cooking, not only on serving day but during your cooking session as well. There are a number of tools that can make quick work of your cooking tasks or even take them off your hands completely, so that you can work on other recipes in your meal plan.

You probably already have basic cookery tools at your disposal, but the following are especially suited to making your bulk cooking sessions more efficient. If there's something on this list you don't own, consider borrowing from a friend for your next cooking session or investing in the item if you have the space to store it.

Slow Cookers. The slow cooker is a home cook's best friend. Who else simmers a stew for you while you turn your attention to other tasks? Using one or two large slow cookers during your cooking session will not only result in several prepared meals, it will also free up valuable stovetop real estate for other dishes.

Large Stockpots. While the slow cooker works on a stew, the stockpot on your stove can be busy with soup or red sauce. It is also helpful for browning large batches of ground beef. Having one or even two large stockpots is helpful when cooking up a storm.

Bread Machine. The bread machine is an efficient kitchen servant that can work wonders. In less than 2 hours, it can prepare dough for 4 pizzas or 32 rolls. Since yeast dough freezes best without long rising times, you can instead run your bread machine through more than one mixing cycle in a short amount of time.

Stand Mixer. A stand mixer is ideal for mashing large batches of potatoes or mixing up mega batches of cookie dough. It can also knead bread dough and whip up a cheesecake in a matter of minutes. A stand mixer can reduce your prep time tremendously.

Food Processor. A food processor is a whiz at shredding cheeses and chopping vegetables quickly, helping you get your food from the grocery bag to the freezer in the shortest time possible. It's also great for blending sauces and soups.

Immersion Blender. An immersion, or stick, blender can quickly puree a smoothie or soup—no need to transfer the mixture to a blender or food processor. It also reduces the number of items to wash, getting you out of the kitchen even faster.

KEEP A FREEZER INVENTORY

After you spend good time and money planning, shopping, and cooking, you want to make sure that you enjoy those frozen assets in a timely manner. Frozen food, properly stored at 0°F (−18°C), will keep indefinitely. But eventually, texture and taste can break down under cold storage.

A good rule of thumb is to consume your frozen meals within two to three months. Good labeling is key, so that you know when you made a certain dish and what that dish is. No mystery meat allowed!

Depending on what kind of freezer storage you are using, you may want to keep track of your freezer meals by posting a list of some kind in a prominent spot. If you cross off the items as you use them and add to the list as you add to your freezer inventory, you should always have a good idea of what meals are available to you. There are even smartphone apps to help you track what you've got!

A Home-Kitchen Assembly Line

Henry Ford probably never dreamed that his assembly-line practices of sequential organization and minimal worker motion would help out a home cook a century later. Ford realized that creating many of the same items in succession saves time and money because the worker is simply repeating a motion many times over instead of starting from scratch each time. The same holds true for bulk cooking.

Assembling a lasagna from start to finish might take 30 minutes. But assembling four lasagnas does not take two hours. Mass production takes less time than making several single items one after another.

By creating a sequence in food prep and having all your ingredients within arm's reach, you can prepare bulk batches of any number of recipes and decrease the effort and time that it takes.

Batch cooking can free you up to have your cake and eat it, too. You can enjoy home-cooked meals any night of the week without a lot of fuss. You don't need to spend a lot of time in the kitchen in order to fill your freezer and make things easier for yourself in the days and weeks ahead. A little efficiency goes a long way.

Work It—for *You*

Freezer cooking can work for any household, budget, or size of freezer. Explore the different modes of packaging, purchasing, and preparation until you find the ones you like the best. With proper planning and equipment, you can easily prepare delicious meals at home, on a budget, and in accord with your own dietary preferences. Make-ahead-and-freeze cooking can enable you to have home-cooked meals whenever you want them, without the marathon cooking sessions of yesteryear.

COVERING THE BASES: SAUCES AND SPICE MIXES

Traditional recipes for freezing usually feature canned soups, prepared sauces, and foil packets of seasoning mixes. While these products are certainly quick and easy to use, they can be expensive and contain dubious ingredients. Creating your own cooking sauces and spice mixes is a great way to have flavor at your fingertips without a lot of fuss—or a lot of fake food.

The following sauces and spice blends are featured in recipes throughout this book. By preparing a bulk batch at the beginning of a cooking session, you can save yourself a great deal of time and ensure that delicious, quality ingredients are incorporated into your meals.

- Beefy Mushroom Gravy, page 25
- Basic Taco Seasoning Mix, page 29
- Chipotle Taco Seasoning Mix, page 30
- Jamie's Spice Mix, page 30
- Easy Slow Cooker Red Sauce, page 89
- Homemade Cream of Celery Soup for Cooking, page 93
- Parmesan Herb Blend, page 130

CHAPTER 1
Where's the Beef?

Chipotle-Rubbed Tri-Tip

For decades on the West Coast, tri-tip has been a favorite grilling cut. It's meaty and full of flavor. Thankfully, meat cutters throughout the country have caught on to what California butchers have long known: The tri-tip is a delicious cut of beef. If you don't see it in the meat case, ask your butcher. You can also use your favorite grilling cut of beef instead. Having the meat and spice rub ready to throw on the grill will help you pull off a great cookout. Serve the roast sliced with fresh salsa.

Packaging: Snack-size zip-top bag, gallon-size (4 L) zip-top freezer bag

1 teaspoon chipotle chile powder

½ teaspoon ground cumin

¼ teaspoon freshly ground black pepper

1 teaspoon fine sea salt

1 teaspoon garlic powder

One 2-pound (908 g) tri-tip roast, in its original packaging

WHEN READY TO SERVE, YOU WILL NEED:

1 tablespoon (15 ml) grapeseed oil or olive oil

Easy Homemade Salsa (page 29)

—
Serves 4 to 8

Combine all the spices in the snack-size bag. Place the tri-tip roast and the bag of spices in the freezer bag.

FREEZING: Store the roast and spice packet in the freezer until a day or two before serving.

TO THAW AND SERVE: Thaw the roast completely on a tray in the refrigerator. Rub the tri-tip with the oil. Rub the seasoning mix into the meat, coating it thoroughly. Cook the roast on a hot grill, turning once, for 40 minutes, or until it reaches the desired doneness; the internal temperature should be 135°F (57°C) for medium-rare or 160°F (71°C) for well done. Allow the roast to rest, tented with foil, for 10 minutes. Slice the meat against the grain and serve with salsa.

Vegetable Bolognese

One summer our CSA provided an abundance of eggplant. This Bolognese was the delicious result of my efforts to use it! Packed with vegetables, the sauce goes nicely over hot cooked noodles or rice and makes the base for a fantastic lasagna.

Packaging: Plastic containers with lids

¼ cup (60 ml) olive oil

1 carrot, peeled and finely chopped

1 eggplant, peeled and chopped into ½-inch (1.3 cm) cubes

1 medium-size onion, coarsely chopped

1 red bell pepper, coarsely chopped

1 medium-size zucchini, coarsely chopped

2 cloves garlic, minced

Salt and freshly ground black pepper

1 pound (454 g) ground beef

3½ cups (825 ml) tomato sauce

One 14.5-ounce (406 g) can diced tomatoes with juices

¼ cup (60 ml) red wine (optional)

3 tablespoons chopped fresh basil or 1 tablespoon dried basil

—
Serves 6 to 8

In a large stockpot, heat the olive oil over medium heat until shimmering. Add the carrot and eggplant and cook for 10 minutes, stirring to prevent the eggplant from sticking.

Add the onion, bell pepper, zucchini, and garlic. Cook for 5 more minutes. Add salt and pepper to taste.

Add the ground beef and cook for about 10 minutes or until the meat is cooked through, stirring often. Add the tomato sauce, tomatoes, red wine (if using), and basil. Add a bit of water if the mixture is too thick.

Adjust the seasonings to taste and bring to a bubble. Reduce the heat, cover, and simmer for 25 minutes.

FREEZING: Divide the sauce into meal-size portions in plastic containers. Chill the sauce in the refrigerator before freezing.

TO THAW AND SERVE: Thaw the sauce in the refrigerator and reheat it in a saucepan.

Beefy Mushroom Gravy

Preceding generations may have relied on canned cream soups and gravies to pull together quick meals. But these soups, chock full of sodium and additives, don't do a lot for us except save some time. In reality, it doesn't take very long to make up a batch of this beef and mushroom gravy. Use it as a simple sauce, in place of cream of mushroom soup, and in recipes like Shepherd's Pie with Green Chile Mashed Potatoes (page 40) and Swedish Meatballs with Dill (page 32). If you are using commercial beef broth, taste the gravy before adding salt, since such broths can vary greatly in their levels of saltiness.

Packaging: Plastic container with lid or pint-size (470 ml) zip-top freezer bag

4½ tablespoons (63 g) unsalted butter, divided

¼ cup (18 g) finely chopped fresh mushrooms

2 tablespoons (16 g) finely chopped onion

¼ cup (30 g) unbleached all-purpose flour

2 cups (470 ml) beef broth

2 teaspoons fresh chopped parsley or ¾ teaspoon dried parsley flakes

¾ teaspoon salt

⅛ teaspoon freshly ground black pepper

⅛ teaspoon paprika

—
Makes about 2 cups (470 ml)

In a medium skillet, melt ½ tablespoon of the butter over medium heat. Add the mushrooms and onion. Sauté the vegetables, stirring occasionally, until the mushrooms start to brown and the onion becomes translucent. Set aside.

In a heavy stockpot, melt the remaining 4 tablespoons (56 g) of butter over medium heat. Stir in the flour and cook, stirring, until the mixture bubbles. Cook for 1 more minute.

Whisk in the beef broth, stirring constantly, until the mixture thickens to a gravy consistency.

Stir in the mushroom and onion mixture, parsley, salt, pepper, and paprika. Adjust the seasonings to taste.

FREEZING: Divide the gravy into desired portions in plastic containers. Chill the gravy in the refrigerator before freezing.

TO THAW AND SERVE: Thaw the gravy in the refrigerator. Reheat in a saucepan over medium heat, whisking to recombine.

NOTE:

To make a big batch of this gravy, simply multiply all the ingredients by four. The cooking method remains the same.

Meatball Sub Kit

Meatball subs are classic comfort food. Skip the trip to the deli by making your own—and better!—subs at home for less. Put together a few meatball sub kits so that you can indulge yourself whenever a craving hits.

Packaging: Plastic containers with lids, gallon- (4 L), quart- (1 L) and sandwich-size zip-top freezer bags.

40 small cooked meatballs (about ½ batch Herbed Meatballs, page 36)

2 cups (470 ml) favorite marinara sauce

½ cup (112 g) butter, softened

1 teaspoon chopped garlic

½ teaspoon dried parsley

8 submarine rolls or hearty hot dog buns

Mozzarella cheese, for topping (optional)

—
Makes 8 sandwiches

Place the cooled, cooked meatballs in a closed container or zip-top bag.

Place the sauce in a closed container or zip-top bag.

In a small mixing bowl, combine the butter, garlic, and parsley. Spread this mixture on both cut sides of the rolls. Wrap the rolls in foil and place in a larger zip-top bag.

Place the cheese in a small zip-top bag.

FREEZING: Place the chilled containers or bags of meatballs, sauce, rolls, and cheese together in the freezer.

TO THAW AND SERVE: Thaw the components in the refrigerator. Reheat the sauce and meatballs in the microwave or in a pan on the stovetop. Bake the wrapped rolls for 10 minutes in a 350°F (180°C or gas mark 4) oven. Unwrap the rolls and open them. Broil the rolls until crisp and golden. Assemble the sandwiches by piling 5 meatballs and your desired amount of sauce on each roll and topping with cheese. Return to the broiler if you'd like to melt the cheese a bit more. Serve immediately.

Not Your Convenience Store's Frozen Burritos

I once turned my nose up at frozen burritos, assuming they would be mushy and blah-tasting. But friends raved about making their own, so I had to try it out. And we loved them! Snacks and dinners come together so easily when the burritos are premade. Crisping them on the griddle takes them to a new level, and you'd never know they'd been frozen.

Packaging: Gallon-size (4 L) zip-top freezer bags

1 pound (454 g) ground beef

1 to 2 tablespoons Basic Taco Seasoning Mix (opposite page)

3 cups (750 g) refried beans

2 cups (240 g) shredded cheddar cheese

1 cup (235 ml) enchilada sauce

½ cup (80 g) diced onion

One 4-ounce (112 g) can chopped green chiles

12 burrito-size flour tortillas

—

Serves 6 to 12

In a large skillet, cook the meat over medium-high heat, stirring frequently, until no pink remains. Stir in the taco seasoning. Stir to blend.

Drain the meat and transfer it to a large bowl. Add the beans, cheese, enchilada sauce, onion, and green chiles. Stir well to combine.

Lay out a tortilla and spread a scant ½ cup filling in a line down one side of the tortilla. Roll the tortilla around the filling, rolling toward the middle of the tortilla. Fold in the sides and continue rolling.

Fill and roll the rest of the burritos in the same manner.

FREEZING: Place the rolled burritos in the freezer bags. Chill in the refrigerator before freezing.

TO THAW AND SERVE: Thaw as many burritos as desired in the refrigerator.

TO REHEAT IN THE MICROWAVE: Cook thawed burritos, flipping once, 1 to 2 minutes per burrito, or until hot. You can also reheat them directly from the freezer, without thawing; just add an additional minute or two of cooking time.

TO REHEAT ON THE GRIDDLE: Cook thawed burritos on a hot griddle until the filling is hot and the tortilla is crisp.

TO REHEAT IN THE OVEN: Preheat the oven to 350°F (180°C or gas mark 4). For crispy, oven-baked burritos, bake thawed burritos for 15 to 20 minutes. For softer burritos, wrap each in foil prior to baking. If the burritos are frozen, increase the cooking time by 5 to 10 minutes.

Basic Taco Seasoning Mix

This taco seasoning is a standard spice blend that can be mixed into ground beef, shredded chicken, soups, or chilis to give them a little punch. It is also delicious mixed into sour cream as a dip and stirred into marinades and dressings.

Packaging: Plastic container with lid or pint-size (470 ml) zip-top freezer bag

¼ cup (30 g) chili powder

2 tablespoons dried oregano

2 tablespoons onion flakes

1 tablespoon (18 g) salt

1 tablespoon garlic powder

1 teaspoon freshly ground black pepper

—
Makes about ⅔ cup (65 g)

Combine all of the ingredients in a small bowl. Place the mixture in an airtight plastic container or freezer bag and store in the freezer.

Easy Homemade Salsa

One 14.5-ounce (406 g) can diced tomatoes with juices

One 14.5-ounce (406 g) can fire-roasted diced tomatoes with juices

1 large handful chopped fresh cilantro

¼ cup (36 g) sliced fresh jalapeño pepper

¼ cup (25 g) chopped scallion

Juice of ½ lime

1 clove garlic

Salt

—
Makes about 4 cups (940 ml)

Combine all of the ingredients in the bowl of a food processor. Pulse until smooth. Season to taste with salt.

Jamie's Spice Mix

My sister Jamie has great taste in food. I love learning from her. This spice mix is based on her special blend, one that she gave as a party favor at her wedding when she married into a large Italian family. Add a few shakes to salad dressing, meat marinades, or French fries. It also goes well on pizza.

Packaging: Pint-size (470 ml) zip-top freezer bag or plastic container with lid

2 tablespoons onion powder

2 tablespoons garlic powder

1½ tablespoons paprika

3 tablespoons chopped fresh basil or 1 tablespoon dried basil

1 tablespoon dried oregano

1 tablespoon (18 g) fine sea salt

2 teaspoons freshly ground black pepper

1 teaspoon celery seeds (optional)

½ teaspoon grated lemon zest

½ teaspoon cayenne pepper

Combine all of the ingredients in a small bowl. Place the mixture in an airtight plastic container or freezer bag and store in the freezer.

—
Makes about ⅔ cup (65 g)

Chipotle Taco Seasoning Mix

Chipotle chiles, which are smoke-dried jalapeño peppers, add a little heat and a smoky flavor to foods. Once difficult to find but now widely available, they are sold canned in adobo sauce or dried in whole or ground form. This seasoning mix can be used in taco meats, chilis, and soups to give them a distinctive chipotle flavor.

Packaging: Plastic container with lid or pint-size (470 ml) zip-top freezer bag

2 tablespoons chipotle chile powder

2 tablespoons onion flakes

1 tablespoon garlic powder

1 tablespoon (18 g) salt

1 tablespoon dried oregano

2 teaspoons ground cumin

Combine all of the ingredients in a small bowl. Place the mixture in an airtight plastic container or freezer bag and store in the freezer.

—
Makes about ½ cup (48 g)

Sweet and Spicy Joes

Sloppy joes can be too sweet for some palates. This variation retains some of the sweet but adds a spicy kick for variety. If you do prefer a sweeter version, simply add more brown sugar.

Packaging: Plastic containers with lids

2 pounds (908 g) ground beef

1 to 2 cups (235 to 470 ml) tomato sauce, depending on how saucy you like it

2½ tablespoons (15 g) Jamie's Spice Mix (opposite page)

1 tablespoon brown sugar

WHEN READY TO SERVE, YOU WILL NEED:

Hamburger buns

Shredded cheddar cheese

Sliced dill pickles

—
Serves 4 to 8

In a large skillet, cook the meat over medium-high heat, stirring frequently, until no pink remains.

Stir in the tomato sauce, spice mix, and brown sugar. Bring to a bubble and then simmer for 20 minutes.

FREEZING: Divide the meat mixture into meal-size portions in plastic containers. Chill in the refrigerator before freezing.

TO THAW AND SERVE: Thaw in the refrigerator. Reheat the mixture in a saucepan. Spoon the hot mixture onto hamburger buns and top with cheese and pickles. Serve immediately.

Swedish Meatballs with Dill

This meatball dish is enjoyed by diners of all ages, particularly when served with mashed potatoes or hot cooked noodles and lingonberry or cranberry sauce. The rich beef gravy will have them licking the plates clean.

Packaging: Quart- (1 L) or gallon-size (4 L) zip-top freezer bags, plastic containers with lids

3 pounds (1362 g) ground beef

1 pound (454 g) ground pork

3 cups (150 g) fresh bread crumbs

6 large eggs, beaten

1 cup (160 g) finely chopped onion

3 cloves garlic, minced

⅓ cup chopped fresh parsley or 2 tablespoons dried parsley flakes

¼ cup chopped fresh dill or 1 tablespoon plus 2 teaspoons dried dill, divided

2 teaspoons kosher salt

¼ teaspoon ground allspice

8 cups (1880 ml) Beefy Mushroom Gravy (page 25)

—
Serves 12 to 16

Line 2 rimmed baking sheets with heavy-duty foil. Spray the foil lightly with nonstick cooking spray. Preheat the oven to 350°F (180°C or gas mark 4).

In a large bowl, mix the ground meats, bread crumbs, eggs, onion, garlic, parsley, 3 tablespoons of the fresh dill or 1 tablespoon of the dried, salt, and allspice just until everything is evenly distributed. Don't overmix, as that will make your meatballs tough.

Form the mixture into golf ball–size balls and place the meatballs on the prepared sheets. Bake the meatballs for 15 minutes, or until they are cooked through.

Pour the gravy into a large bowl. Add the remaining dill and stir to combine.

FREEZING: Divide the meatballs into meal-size portions in freezer bags. Divide the gravy into plastic containers. Chill the meatballs and gravy in the refrigerator before freezing.

TO THAW AND SERVE: Thaw the meatballs and gravy in the refrigerator. Reheat the gravy in a large saucepan on the stovetop, whisking to recombine. Add the meatballs and simmer until heated through. Serve immediately.

Soy-Balsamic Burgers

Burgers are a go-to supper any time of year, but particularly during the warmer months; there's something so inviting about meat that has been cooked over an open flame. Having a stash of patties in the freezer makes your prep time even quicker. These burgers are seasoned with balsamic vinegar and soy sauce, adding delicious flavor to the meat.

Packaging: Gallon-size (4 L) zip-top freezer bag, waxed paper, plastic wrap

2 pounds (908 g) ground beef

1 tablespoon (15 ml) balsamic vinegar

1 tablespoon (15 ml) soy sauce

1 tablespoon chopped fresh parsley or 1 teaspoon dried parsley flakes

½ teaspoon dried thyme

¼ teaspoon freshly ground black pepper

WHEN READY TO SERVE, YOU WILL NEED:

Hamburger buns

Lettuce leaves or shredded lettuce

Sliced tomatoes

Other toppings, as desired

—
Serves 8

In a large bowl, mix all of the ingredients just until everything is evenly distributed. Don't overmix, as that will make your burgers tough.

Divide the mixture into 8 equal portions. Form each portion into a flat hamburger patty.

FREEZING: Place the patties on a baking sheet and freeze until firm. Remove the frozen patties from the sheet and place them in a freezer bag. Seal the bag carefully, removing as much air as possible. Return the burgers to the freezer. Alternatively, you can freeze the burgers in meal-size bundles, separating the patties with waxed paper. Wrap each bundle in plastic wrap and place in a freezer bag.

TO THAW AND SERVE: If you have frozen your hamburger patties individually, simply remove the desired number of patties from the bag. There is no need to thaw them before cooking. If you used the bundle method of packaging, thaw the bundle on a dish in the refrigerator. (You may be able to cook these unthawed as well, if the frozen patties separate easily.) Place the hamburger patties on a hot grill or in a skillet. When the tops of the burgers appear wet, flip them over. Continue cooking until the burgers reach the desired doneness. Serve on buns with lettuce, tomatoes, and other toppings as desired.

Outside-In Cheeseburgers

Join two great tastes in one by mixing your cheese into this outside-in cheeseburger. The added dill is reminiscent of dill pickles, making this truly an all-in-one burger.

Packaging: Gallon-size (4 L) zip-top freezer bag, waxed paper, plastic wrap

2 pounds (908 g) ground beef

½ cup (80 g) finely chopped onion

½ cup (60 g) shredded cheddar cheese

1½ teaspoons fresh chopped dill or ½ teaspoon dried dill

½ teaspoon salt

¼ teaspoon freshly ground black pepper

WHEN READY TO SERVE, YOU WILL NEED:

Hamburger buns

Lettuce leaves or shredded lettuce

Sliced tomatoes

Other toppings, as desired

—
Serves 8

In a large bowl, mix all of the ingredients just until everything is evenly distributed. Don't overmix, as that will make your burgers tough.

Divide the mixture into 8 equal portions. Form each portion into a flat hamburger patty.

FREEZING: Place the patties on a baking sheet and freeze until firm. Remove the frozen patties from the sheet and place them in a freezer bag. Seal the bag carefully, removing as much air as possible. Return the burgers to the freezer. Alternatively, you can freeze the burgers in meal-size bundles, separating the patties with waxed paper. Wrap each bundle in plastic wrap and place in a freezer bag.

TO THAW AND SERVE: If you have frozen your hamburger patties individually, simply remove the desired number of patties from the bag. There is no need to thaw them before cooking. If you used the bundle method of packaging, thaw the bundle on a dish in the refrigerator. (You may be able to cook these unthawed as well, if the frozen patties separate easily.) Place the hamburger patties on a hot grill or in a skillet. When the tops of the burgers appear wet, flip them over. Continue cooking until the burgers reach the desired doneness. Serve on buns with lettuce, tomatoes, and other toppings as desired.

Herbed Meatballs

Meatballs are one of the handiest meal components to keep in the freezer. They can be added to soup, served atop a bowl of spaghetti, dressed in gravy over mashed potatoes, basted with barbecue sauce on the grill, or spooned into a crusty roll with red sauce for a fabulous hot sandwich. You can even serve them as meatball sliders on small dinner rolls. This recipe is easy—and just waiting to be finished with your favorite sauce.

Packaging: Quart- (1 L) or gallon-size (4 L) zip-top freezer bags

4 pounds (1816 g) ground beef

3 cups (150 g) fresh bread crumbs

6 large eggs, beaten

1 cup (160 g) chopped onion

⅓ cup chopped fresh parsley or 2 tablespoons dried parsley flakes

3 tablespoons chopped fresh basil or 1 tablespoon dried basil

3 cloves garlic, chopped

1 teaspoon kosher salt

—
Serves 12 to 16

Line two rimmed baking sheets with heavy-duty foil. Spray the foil lightly with nonstick cooking spray. Preheat the oven to 350°F (180°C or gas mark 4).

In a large bowl, mix all of the ingredients just until everything is evenly distributed. Don't overmix, as that will make your meatballs tough.

Form the mixture into golf ball–size balls and place the meatballs on the prepared sheets. Bake the meatballs for 15 minutes, or until they are cooked through.

FREEZING: Divide the meatballs into meal-size portions in freezer bags. Chill the bags in the refrigerator before freezing.

TO THAW AND SERVE: Thaw the meatballs in the refrigerator. Reheat them in your choice of sauce on the stovetop.

Herbed Meatloaf

The basic meatball mixture can also be formed into four meatloaves. Lay out four large sheets of aluminum foil. Divide the meat mixture into four portions, placing one portion on each sheet of foil. Form each of the four portions into a loaf. Wrap each loaf well with the aluminum foil and place them into labeled zip-top freezer bags. Freeze.

TO THAW AND SERVE: Thaw the meatloaf completely in the refrigerator. Preheat the oven to 350°F (180°C or gas mark 4). Unwrap the meatloaf, place it on a baking sheet, and bake for 45 to 60 minutes or until cooked through.

Barbecue Sauce for Meatballs

Add a little smoky flavor to meatballs by warming them on a hot grill and basting them with this super-spicy sauce. For less heat, reduce the cayenne pepper. Serve over mashed potatoes or hot cooked noodles.

Packaging: 1-cup (235 ml) plastic containers with lids

2 tablespoons (30 ml) olive oil

1 cup (160 g) finely chopped onion

4 cloves garlic, minced

2 cups (470 ml) tomato sauce

½ cup (120 ml) apple cider vinegar

¼ cup (56 g) dark brown sugar

1 tablespoon chipotle chile powder

1 teaspoon cayenne pepper, or to taste

⅛ teaspoon crushed red pepper flakes

⅛ teaspoon ground ginger

⅛ teaspoon ground cloves

⅛ teaspoon dry mustard

⅛ teaspoon ground cinnamon

—
Makes about 2 cups (470 ml)

In a large saucepan, heat the oil over medium heat. Add the onion and garlic and cook for 8 minutes, or until the onion is tender and starting to caramelize.

Add all of the remaining ingredients and stir until well-combined. Bring to a low boil, stirring constantly. Reduce the heat, cover, and simmer for 30 minutes, stirring occasionally.

Blend the sauce with an immersion blender or in a food processor until smooth.

FREEZING: Divide the sauce into 1-cup (235 ml) plastic containers. Chill the sauce in the refrigerator before freezing.

TO THAW AND SERVE: Thaw the sauce in the refrigerator. Reheat in the microwave or in a pan on the stovetop. Serve as a sauce for meatballs, hot or at room temperature.

Boules de Picolat (Catalan Meatballs)

This dish is best made with porcini mushrooms, also known as *cèpes*, but I've replaced them with the more easily located and economical button mushrooms. Feel free to use your favorite variety.

Packaging: Quart- (1 L) or gallon-size (4 L) zip-top freezer bags

3 pounds (1362 g) ground beef

1 pound (454 g) ground pork

2 cups (320 g) chopped onion, divided

3 tablespoons chopped fresh parsley or 1 tablespoon dried parsley flakes

3 cloves garlic, chopped

1 teaspoon salt

½ teaspoon freshly ground black pepper

2 tablespoons (30 ml) olive oil

½ cup (35 g) coarsely chopped fresh mushrooms

Two 28-ounce (784 g) cans crushed tomatoes in puree

One 14.5-ounce (406 g) can diced tomatoes with juices

WHEN READY TO SERVE, YOU WILL NEED:

1 cup (100 g) green Spanish olives with pimientos

Boiled potatoes or steamed rice

—
Serves 12 to 16

Line two rimmed baking sheets with heavy-duty foil. Spray the foil lightly with nonstick cooking spray. Preheat the oven to 350°F (180°C or gas mark 4).

In a large bowl, mix the meats, 1 cup (160 g) of the onion, parsley, garlic, salt, and pepper until everything is evenly distributed. Don't overmix, as that will make your meatballs tough.

Form the mixture into golf ball–size balls and place the meatballs on the prepared sheets. Bake the meatballs for 15 minutes, or until they are cooked through.

In a large stockpot, heat the oil over medium-high heat until shimmering. Add the mushrooms and the remaining 1 cup (160 g) chopped onion to the pot. Cook, stirring, until the onion becomes translucent and the mushrooms start to brown slightly, about 5 minutes. Stir in the crushed tomatoes and diced tomatoes.

Add the cooked meatballs to the pot and stir well. Simmer the mixture for 20 minutes.

FREEZING: Divide the meatballs and sauce into meal-size portions in freezer bags. Chill the meatballs and sauce in the refrigerator before storing in the freezer.

TO THAW AND SERVE: Thaw in the refrigerator. Reheat the meatballs and sauce in a saucepan. Stir in the olives and cook until heated through. Serve immediately, along with the potatoes.

Shepherd's Pie with Green Chile Mashed Potatoes

Shepherd's pie is a traditional English dish, made of a ground meat-and-vegetable mixture that's topped with mashed potatoes. This one is spiced up with jalapeños, cilantro, and cheddar cheese, giving it a little South of the Border flavor.

Packaging: 9 × 13-inch (23 × 33 cm) baking dish with lid

8 medium-size red potatoes (about 2 pounds [908 g]), scrubbed and quartered (no need to peel, unless you prefer them that way)

1 pound (454 g) ground beef

1 cup (160 g) chopped onion

½ cup (75 g) chopped red bell pepper

1 tablespoon finely chopped fresh jalapeño pepper

2 cups (470 ml) Beefy Mushroom Gravy (page 25)

1 cup (150 g) fresh or frozen green peas

⅓ cup chopped fresh cilantro

1 teaspoon ground cumin

¼ cup (56 g) (½ stick) salted butter

2 tablespoons (30 ml) half-and-half

½ cup (60 g) shredded cheddar cheese

1 tablespoon canned green chiles

—
Serves 6 to 8

Grease the baking dish. In a large pot of boiling salted water, cook the potatoes until tender, then drain. Set aside.

Meanwhile, in a large skillet, cook the beef, onion, bell pepper, and jalapeño over medium-high heat until the meat is cooked and the vegetables are tender. Drain the meat and vegetables and transfer the mixture to a large bowl.

Add the gravy, peas, cilantro, and cumin. Stir gently to combine. Spread the meat mixture in the prepared pan.

Mash the potatoes with a potato masher until smooth. Blend in the butter. Stir in the half-and-half until smooth. Add the cheddar cheese and green chiles, and stir until well combined.

Spoon the mashed potatoes over the meat mixture, spreading to cover evenly.

FREEZING: Cover the dish and chill in the refrigerator before freezing.

TO THAW AND SERVE: Thaw the casserole in the refrigerator. Preheat the oven to 350°F (180°C or gas mark 4). Bake for 1 hour, until the filling is bubbly and the mashed potatoes are golden brown.

Vegetable-Beef Lasagna

Lasagna is a faithful friend to a freezer cook. This delicious version features cream cheese in the filling, a technique used by cookbook author Ann Hodgman. Use uncooked noodles for even quicker prep time. With an adequate amount of sauce, the uncooked noodles will soften during freezing and cook during baking.

Packaging: 9 × 13-inch (23 × 33 cm) baking dish with lid

3 cups (675 g) Vegetable Bolognese (page 24) or other favorite sauce

3 cups (360 g) shredded mozzarella cheese

8 regular (not no-boil) lasagna noodles, uncooked

8 ounces (224 g) Neufchâtel cheese

1 cup (235 ml) chicken broth

—
Serves 6 to 8

Grease the baking dish. Spread 1½ cups (337 g) of the Bolognese sauce across the bottom of the pan. Sprinkle 1 cup (120 g) of the mozzarella cheese over the sauce. Lay 4 lasagna noodles across the cheese, overlapping slightly.

In a medium saucepan, heat the cream cheese and chicken broth over low heat. As the cream cheese begins to warm and soften, whisk it into the chicken broth until well blended. Pour this mixture over the noodle layer. Sprinkle 1 cup (120 g) of the mozzarella cheese over the white sauce. Lay the remaining 4 lasagna noodles across the layer of cheese.

Spoon the remaining Bolognese over the noodles and spread evenly. Top the sauce with the remaining 1 cup (120 g) mozzarella cheese.

FREEZING: Cover the pan and chill completely in the refrigerator before freezing.

TO THAW AND SERVE: Thaw the lasagna in the refrigerator overnight for best results. Preheat the oven to 400°F (200°C or gas mark 6). Bake for 45 minutes or until the sauce is bubbly and the cheese is melted. Allow the lasagna to rest for 10 minutes before cutting and serving.

CHAPTER 2
Winning Chicken and Surf Dinners

Basic Herb-Baked Chicken

You can maximize your savings by using bone-in chicken breasts. They often go on sale, making them a very economical protein; stock up and bake a bulk batch to have on hand. I prefer bone-in chicken breasts because the meat tends to be more flavorful and doesn't dry out the way boneless, skinless chicken breasts sometimes do.

Packaging: Quart-size (1 L) zip-top freezer bags or quart-size (1 L) plastic containers with lids

6 bone-in chicken breasts

1 teaspoon fine sea salt

1 teaspoon garlic powder

½ teaspoon freshly ground black pepper

1 teaspoon *herbes de Provence*, chili powder, or mixed Italian herbs (optional)

—

Makes at least 6 cups (840 g) chopped cooked chicken

Preheat the oven to 375°F (190°C or gas mark 5).

Place three chicken breasts in each of two 9 × 13-inch (23 × 33 cm) baking dishes. Sprinkle the chicken with salt, garlic powder, pepper, and seasoning, if using.

Bake the chicken for 45 minutes to 1 hour, or until the juices run clear when the chicken is pierced with a knife.

Remove the chicken from the pan and set aside until cool enough to handle.

Remove the chicken meat from the bones.

Chop or shred the chicken, as desired.

FREEZING: If using the chicken in a recipe, proceed with the recipe. Otherwise, place the cooked chicken in freezer bags or containers. Chill the chicken in the refrigerator before freezing.

TO THAW AND SERVE: Thaw the chicken in the refrigerator. Use as desired in recipes.

Simply Poached Chicken

The two tricks to tender poached chicken are to avoid boiling it and to allow it to cool in the pan. This method lends itself well to a freezer-cooking session. Get the pan of chicken started, simmer for the allotted time, and then turn it off. While it cools, you can work on other cooking tasks.

Packaging: Quart-size (1 L) zip-top freezer bags or quart-size (1 L) plastic containers with lids

2 pounds (908 g) boneless, skinless chicken breasts or tenders

2 bay leaves

4 black peppercorns

1 clove garlic, peeled

—

Makes about 4 cups (560 g) chopped cooked chicken

In a large pot, combine the chicken, bay leaves, peppercorns, garlic, and enough water to cover the chicken by at least 1 inch (2.5 cm). Heat the water just to a boil.

Turn down the heat and simmer for 15 to 20 minutes, or until the chicken reaches an internal temperature of 165°F (74°C).

Turn off the heat and allow the chicken to cool in the liquid.

Chop or shred the cooked chicken, as desired.

FREEZING: If using the chicken in a recipe, proceed with the recipe. Otherwise, place the cooked chicken in freezer bags or containers. Chill the chicken in the refrigerator before freezing.

TO THAW AND SERVE: Thaw the chicken in the refrigerator. Use as desired in recipes.

Spicy Southwest Chicken

This marinade is almost like a salsa. It's full of fresh flavors that miraculously withstand the cold of the freezer and come shining through later. Any leftover grilled chicken can be chopped and served in tacos or atop salads.

Packaging: Gallon-size (4 L) zip-top freezer bag

1 medium-size tomato, quartered

½ medium-size onion, cut into chunks

¼ cup (60 ml) vegetable oil

¼ cup (60 ml) soy sauce

¼ cup fresh cilantro leaves

¼ to ½ jalapeño pepper, chopped, to taste

2 cloves garlic

1 tablespoon (15 ml) freshly squeezed lime juice

4 to 6 boneless, skinless chicken breasts

—

Serves 4 to 6

Place the freezer bag in a medium bowl, folding the top over the edges.

In a blender or in a food processor fitted with a metal blade, combine the tomato, onion, oil, soy sauce, cilantro, jalapeño, garlic, and lime juice. Blend until smooth.

Pour the marinade into the prepared bag. Add the chicken pieces. Seal the bag and massage it gently to combine and distribute the ingredients.

Marinate for 2 to 8 hours in the refrigerator if cooking the same day, or freeze immediately.

FREEZING: Freeze the bag flat in the freezer.

TO THAW AND SERVE: A day or two before serving, remove the bag from the freezer and place it on a tray or dish to thaw in the refrigerator. Grill the thawed chicken breasts over a hot fire, turning once, until cooked through.

Mahi Mahi with Almond-Lime Butter

Whenever I serve this simple fish with almond-lime butter, folks just can't get enough of it. With the flavors and textures of lime zest, toasted almonds, and dill, this butter sauce blends delectably into the fish. This is my mom's favorite recipe in this entire book!

Packaging: Plastic wrap, gallon-size (4 L) zip-top freezer bag

4 mahi mahi fillets, 5 to 8 ounces (140 to 224 g) each, wrapped securely in freezer paper

½ cup (112 g) (1 stick) salted butter, softened

¼ cup (27 g) toasted sliced almonds

1½ teaspoons chopped fresh dill or ½ teaspoon dried dill

Grated zest of 1 lime

½ teaspoon kosher salt

Freshly ground black pepper

—
Serves 4

Place the fish in the freezer bag. Place the bag in the freezer.

In a small bowl, combine the softened butter, almonds, dill, lime zest, salt, and pepper. Blend well.

Lay out a small sheet of plastic wrap. Spoon the compound butter onto the center of the plastic wrap. Using the plastic wrap as a guide, form the butter into a narrow log. Wrap the butter securely in the plastic wrap and place the butter log in the freezer bag with the fish. Seal and return the bag to the freezer.

TO THAW AND SERVE: Thaw the bag in the refrigerator. Season the thawed fillets with salt and pepper and cook them, turning once, on a hot, oiled grill for 10 to 15 minutes or until the fish starts to flake. Meanwhile, allow the butter to soften. Top each fillet with a few slices of the compound butter. The butter will melt quickly on top of the hot fish, forming a sauce. Serve immediately.

Spicy Dijon Chicken

Who would have thought that five ingredients could get together and throw a veritable party in your mouth? This Dijon chicken, loosely adapted from one in an old Williams-Sonoma grilling cookbook, pulls that off. Though I highly doubt my French maman would have ever added cayenne to her chicken, the Dijon and the pepper combine to give this dish a great kick. You can adjust the heat by increasing or reducing the amount of cayenne; be aware that it will taste spicier once it's cooked.

Packaging: Gallon-size (4 L) zip-top freezer bag

⅓ cup (42 g) Dijon mustard

¼ cup (60 ml) olive oil

2 tablespoons (30 ml) red wine vinegar

1 teaspoon cayenne pepper

4 to 6 boneless, skinless chicken breasts

—
Serves 4 to 6

Place the freezer bag in a medium bowl, folding the top over the edges.

In a small bowl, combine the Dijon mustard, oil, vinegar, and cayenne. Whisk to blend.

Pour the marinade into the prepared bag. Add the chicken pieces. Seal the bag and massage gently to combine and distribute the ingredients.

Marinate for 2 to 8 hours in the refrigerator if cooking the same day, or freeze immediately.

FREEZING: Freeze the bag flat in the freezer.

TO THAW AND SERVE: A day or two before serving, remove the bag from the freezer and place it on a tray or dish to thaw in the refrigerator. Grill the thawed chicken breasts over a hot fire, turning once, until cooked through.

Tandoori Chicken

Teaching my children at home, I've learned about different cultures and their recipes. I wasn't sure my kids would go for tandoori chicken, but I was pleasantly surprised when they loved it. The spices gain strength in the freezer, so I've reduced the amount of seasoning that I would normally use for cooking it fresh.

Packaging: Gallon-size (4 L) zip-top freezer bag

¾ cup (180 g) low-fat plain yogurt or buttermilk

2 tablespoons (30 ml) freshly squeezed lemon juice

1 tablespoon (15 ml) olive oil

1 teaspoon paprika

1 teaspoon minced fresh ginger

1 teaspoon curry powder

1 clove garlic, finely chopped

½ teaspoon salt

½ teaspoon chili powder

4 to 6 boneless, skinless chicken breasts

(continued)

Serves 4 to 6

Place the freezer bag in a medium bowl, folding the top over the edges. Combine the yogurt, lemon juice, olive oil, paprika, ginger, curry powder, garlic, salt, and chili powder in the bag. Swirl the bowl gently or use a whisk to combine.

Add the chicken pieces. Seal the bag and massage gently to combine and distribute the ingredients.

Marinate for 2 to 8 hours in the refrigerator if cooking the same day, or freeze immediately.

FREEZING: Freeze the bag flat in the freezer.

TO THAW AND SERVE: A day or two before serving, remove the bag from the freezer and place it on a tray or dish to thaw in the refrigerator. Grill the thawed chicken breasts over a hot fire, turning once, until cooked through.

Easy Caesar Salad with Garlicky Italian Grilled Chicken

In some ways, this is a "mock" Caesar salad. Gone are the raw egg and anchovies. But the dressing still packs quite a punch, and it comes together quickly, making it an ideal accent to a freezer meal.

Juice of 1 lemon (about ¼ cup [60 ml])

1 clove garlic, minced

½ cup (120 ml) olive oil

Salt and freshly ground black pepper

2 to 3 Garlicky Italian Chicken Breasts (page 50)

1 head romaine lettuce, torn into bite-size pieces and refrigerated until ready to serve

¾ cup (75 g) freshly grated Parmesan cheese

1 cup (50 g) Croutons

In a small glass jar or bowl, combine the lemon juice and garlic. Blend well. Add the olive oil and shake or whisk well to combine. Season the dressing to taste with salt and pepper.

Slice the chicken breasts across the grain.

In a large salad bowl, toss the lettuce with the dressing. Sprinkle on the cheese and croutons and toss again. Divide the lettuce mixture among serving plates, and top each with a sliced chicken breast. Serve immediately.

Serves 4 to 6

Garlicky Italian Chicken Breasts

Grill up this garlicky chicken one night to serve as a main dish, reserving a couple of pieces to chop and toss on Easy Caesar Salad (previous page) the next night. Get two meals from one recipe, with a minimum amount of work.

Packaging: Gallon-size (4 L) zip-top freezer bag

¼ cup (60 ml) red wine vinegar

¼ cup (60 ml) white wine or sherry

¼ cup (60 ml) olive oil

2 cloves garlic, crushed

1 tablespoon chopped fresh basil or 1 teaspoon dried basil

½ teaspoon dried oregano

¼ teaspoon freshly ground black pepper

Pinch of sugar

4 to 6 boneless, skinless chicken breasts

—

Serves 4 to 6

Place the freezer bag in a medium bowl, folding the top over the edges. Combine the vinegar, white wine, oil, garlic, basil, oregano, pepper, and sugar in the bag. Swirl the bowl gently to combine the ingredients.

Add the chicken pieces. Seal the bag and massage gently to combine and distribute the ingredients.

Marinate for 2 to 8 hours in the refrigerator if cooking the same day, or freeze immediately.

FREEZING: Freeze the bag flat in the freezer.

TO THAW AND SERVE: A day or two before serving, remove the bag from the freezer and place it on a tray or dish to thaw in the refrigerator. Grill the thawed chicken breasts over a hot fire, turning once, until cooked through.

Chicken Enchilada Bake
with Green Chiles and Jalapeños

Early in our marriage, my husband made it clear that he did not care for canned cream-of-anything soup. Imagine my chagrin, as the majority of the recipes I grew up on started with canned soups. Over time, I've learned tastier and healthier ways to make our meals—without the help of canned soups. This enchilada bake would traditionally contain cream of chicken or cream of celery soup. A homemade version, however, takes only a few minutes longer to prepare on the stovetop. This casserole gets an extra kick from green chiles.

Packaging: Two 8-inch (20.3 cm) baking dishes with lids or one 9 × 13-inch (23 × 33 cm) baking dish with lid

3 cups (360 g) shredded cheddar or Monterey Jack cheese, divided

2 cups (470 ml) Homemade Cream of Celery Soup for Cooking (page 93)

1 cup (225 g) sour cream

One 4-ounce (112 g) can chopped green chiles

½ cup (80 g) chopped onion

1 fresh jalapeño pepper, seeded and finely chopped (optional)

2 teaspoons chili powder

12 corn tortillas, cut into bite-size pieces

3 cups (420 g) chopped cooked chicken

—
Serves 6 to 8

Grease the baking dish(es).

In a large bowl, combine 2 cups (240 g) of the cheese, the celery soup, sour cream, green chiles, onion, jalapeño (if using), and chili powder. Mix well.

Stir in the tortillas and the chicken. Spoon the mixture into the prepared baking dish(es).

Sprinkle the casserole(s) with the remaining 1 cup (120 g) cheese.

FREEZING: Cover the dish(es) and chill in the refrigerator before freezing.

TO THAW AND SERVE: Thaw completely in the refrigerator. Preheat the oven to 350°F (180°C or gas mark 4). Bake for 1 hour, or until hot and bubbly.

Chicken-Bacon Subs

Succulent chicken, crisp bacon, melted cheese, and rich garlic butter present a feast for the senses in this sandwich. Certainly, sandwiches aren't difficult to prepare. But knowing that a large gourmet sub is waiting at home, ready to be popped in the oven, is likely to deter us from stopping for fast food. Get a large, soft, Italian-style loaf for this sub, not a crusty baguette-style bread.

Packaging: Heavy-duty aluminum foil

1 large loaf Italian-style bread, 14 to 16 inches (25.6 to 40.6 cm) in length

½ cup (112 g) Garlic Butter (recipe follows)

2 cups (280 g) shredded cooked chicken

¼ cup (20 g) chopped bacon, cooked until crisp

5 ounces (140 g) sliced mozzarella or Monterey Jack cheese

—

Serves 4

Slice the bread in half horizontally and place the halves on a large sheet of heavy-duty aluminum foil. Spread the garlic butter on the bottom half of the bread.

Arrange the shredded chicken on top of the garlic butter. Sprinkle the chicken with the chopped bacon. Layer the cheese over the top.

Place the top half of the bread over the cheese.

FREEZING: Wrap the sub tightly in foil and freeze.

TO THAW AND SERVE: Thaw the sub completely in the refrigerator. Preheat the oven to 350°F (180°C or gas mark 4). Bake the sub for 25 to 30 minutes, until the cheese is melted and the filling is hot. Remove the foil and slice into four portions.

Garlic Butter

½ cup (112 g) unsalted butter, softened

2 cloves garlic, chopped

1½ teaspoons chopped fresh parsley or ½ teaspoon dried parsley flakes

—

Makes ½ cup (112 g)

In a small bowl, combine all of the ingredients. Blend well.

Spicy Taco Lasagna

This turkey lasagna is an interesting twist on a classic, featuring spicy cheese and salsa as well as cream cheese in the filling. Hats off to cookbook author Ann Hodgman for the cream cheese sauce; it's the best. There's no need to cook the noodles, as they will soften during freezing and while the lasagna cooks in the oven. Serve this with sour cream, cilantro, and sliced avocado.

Packaging: 9 × 13-inch (23 × 33 cm) baking dish with lid

1 pound (454 g) ground turkey

2 cups (240 g) shredded pepper jack cheese

2 cups (240 g) shredded cheddar cheese

3 cups (705 ml) Easy Slow Cooker Red Sauce (page 89) or other favorite red sauce

1 cup (235 ml) Easy Homemade Salsa (page 29) or other favorite salsa

1 cup (235 ml) chicken broth

8 ounces (224 g) cream cheese

6 to 8 regular (not no-boil) lasagna noodles

WHEN READY TO SERVE, YOU WILL NEED:

Sour cream

Sliced avocado

Chopped fresh cilantro

—
Serves 6 to 8

In a large skillet over medium-high heat, brown the ground turkey, breaking it up as it cooks, until it is no longer pink. Drain if necessary.

In a bowl, combine the shredded cheeses. In another bowl, combine the browned turkey, red sauce, and salsa.

In a medium saucepan, bring the chicken broth to a simmer. Add the cream cheese and whisk until smooth. Set aside.

Spray the baking dish with nonstick cooking spray. Spread half the turkey mixture in the bottom of the dish. Sprinkle with 1 cup (120 g) of the cheese.

Arrange 3 or 4 of the uncooked lasagna noodles over the cheese layer, breaking them as necessary to fit. Pour the cream cheese mixture over the noodles. Sprinkle with 1 cup (120 g) of the cheese.

Arrange the remaining lasagna noodles over the cream cheese layer. Spread the remaining turkey mixture over the noodles. Sprinkle on the remaining cheese.

FREEZING: Cover the cooled dish and chill in the refrigerator before freezing.

TO THAW AND SERVE: Thaw the lasagna completely in the refrigerator. Preheat the oven to 350°F (180°C or gas mark 4) and bake for 45 minutes to 1 hour, until brown and bubbly. Allow the lasagna to rest for 10 minutes before cutting. Top each serving with sour cream, sliced avocado, and chopped cilantro.

Turkey Burgers with Scallions

Turkey burgers, when well seasoned, are an excellent alternative to traditional hamburgers. These burgers are tender and juicy. Ground turkey is rather sticky, making it difficult to form. Using wet hands to shape the patties will help.

Packaging: Zip-top freezer bags, waxed paper, plastic wrap

1¼ pounds (568 g) ground turkey

½ cup (25 g) fresh bread crumbs

¼ cup (25 g) finely chopped scallions

1 tablespoon (15 ml) sherry

1 teaspoon salt

½ teaspoon freshly ground black pepper

WHEN READY TO SERVE, YOU WILL NEED:

Hamburger buns

Lettuce leaves or shredded lettuce

Sliced tomatoes

Other toppings, as desired

—

Serves 4

In a large bowl, mix all of the ingredients just until everything is evenly distributed. Don't overmix, as that will make your burgers tough.

Divide the mixture into 4 equal portions. Form each portion into a flat patty.

FREEZING: Place the patties on a baking sheet and freeze until firm. Remove the frozen patties from the sheet and place them in a freezer bag. Seal the bag carefully, removing as much air as possible. Return the burgers to the freezer. Alternatively, you can freeze the burgers in meal-size bundles, separating the patties with waxed paper. Wrap each bundle in plastic wrap and place in a freezer bag.

TO THAW AND SERVE: If you have frozen your hamburger patties individually, simply remove the desired number of patties from the bag. There is no need to thaw them before cooking. If you used the bundle method of packaging, thaw the bundle on a dish in the refrigerator. (You may be able to cook these unthawed as well, if the frozen patties separate easily.) Place the hamburger patties on a hot grill or in a skillet. When the tops of the burgers appear wet, flip them over. Continue cooking until the burgers reach the desired doneness. Serve on buns with lettuce, tomatoes, and other toppings as desired.

Got Turkey?

Cooked turkey can often be used in place of cooked chicken in recipes. While turkey has a richer flavor, it is just as freezer-friendly as its barnyard counterpart. Try turkey in one of these recipes as a great way to use up holiday leftovers.

Chicken Enchilada Bake with Green Chiles and Jalapeños, page 51

Chicken-Bacon Subs, page 52

Creamy Chicken Enchiladas, page 59

Chipotle Chicken and Onion Wraps, page 61

Tarragon Turkey Burgers with Blue Cheese and Chipotle Mayo

Chipotle mayonnaise and flavorful blue cheese crown these herbed burgers. No one will miss the all-beef patty.

Packaging: Zip-top freezer bags, waxed paper, plastic wrap

1¼ pounds (568 g) ground turkey

¼ cup (25 g) chopped scallions

1½ teaspoons chopped fresh tarragon leaves or ½ teaspoon dried tarragon

½ teaspoon kosher salt

¼ teaspoon freshly ground black pepper

WHEN READY TO SERVE, YOU WILL NEED:

½ cup (60 g) crumbled blue cheese

½ cup (112 g) mayonnaise

1 chipotle chile in adobo sauce, finely chopped

Hamburger buns

Lettuce leaves or shredded lettuce

Sliced tomatoes

Sliced red onion

Other toppings, as desired

—

Serves 4

In a large bowl, mix all of the ingredients just until everything is evenly distributed. Don't overmix, as that will make your burgers tough.

Divide the mixture into 4 equal portions. Form each portion into a flat patty.

FREEZING: Place the patties on a baking sheet and freeze until firm. Remove the frozen patties from the sheet and place them in a freezer bag. Seal the bag carefully, removing as much air as possible. Return the burgers to the freezer. Alternatively, you can freeze the burgers in meal-size bundles, separating the patties with waxed paper. Wrap each bundle in plastic wrap and place in a freezer bag.

TO THAW AND SERVE: If you have frozen your hamburger patties individually, simply remove the desired number of patties from the bag. There is no need to thaw them before cooking. If you used the bundle method of packaging, thaw the bundle on a dish in the refrigerator. (You may be able to cook these unthawed as well, if the frozen patties separate easily.) Place the hamburger patties on a hot grill or in a skillet. When the tops of the burgers appear wet, flip them over. Continue cooking until the burgers reach the desired doneness.

Top the patties with the blue cheese and allow it to melt slightly before removing the burgers from the heat. In a small bowl, combine the mayonnaise with the chopped chipotle chile and its sauce. Serve the burgers on buns with the mayonnaise, lettuce, tomato, red onion, and other toppings as desired.

Grilled Tilapia or Shrimp Tacos

Fish or shrimp tacos are a delicious twist on Mexican food. Popular in Baja California, they are often served with fresh cabbage and a delectable white sauce. Fried fish is popular as a taco filling, but grilling the seafood is easier and healthier. Package this meal as a kit to be assembled and cooked right before serving.

Packaging: Gallon-size (4 L) zip-top freezer bag, snack-size bag

1 pound (454 g) tilapia fillets or medium-size shrimp (31 to 40 count), peeled and deveined, wrapped securely in freezer paper

1 tablespoon paprika

1 teaspoon sesame seeds

½ teaspoon ground ginger

½ teaspoon freshly ground black pepper

1½ teaspoons chopped fresh dill or ½ teaspoon dried dill

½ teaspoon salt

¼ teaspoon cayenne pepper

WHEN READY TO SERVE, YOU WILL NEED:

1 tablespoon (15 ml) olive oil

Corn tortillas, warmed

Shredded green or red cabbage

Chopped fresh cilantro

Easy Homemade Salsa (page 29)

Lime wedges

—

Serves 4

Place the fish fillets or shrimp in the freezer bag. Place in the freezer.

In a small bowl, combine the paprika, sesame seeds, ginger, pepper, dill, salt, and cayenne. Place the spice mixture in the snack-size bag and place this bag in the larger bag in the freezer.

TO THAW AND SERVE: Thaw the bag in the refrigerator. Brush the thawed fillets or shrimp with the olive oil and sprinkle with the seasoning. Cook the seafood on a hot grill or in a stovetop grill pan, turning once, until the fish starts to flake or the shrimp are pink, 7 to 10 minutes. Assemble the tacos by placing a small portion of seafood on each tortilla. Top the fish with shredded cabbage and chopped cilantro. Serve with salsa and lime wedges.

Creamy Chicken Enchiladas

These creamy enchiladas are full of flavor and texture, with a little punch from the chipotle, pepper jack cheese, and salsa verde, a tangy creaminess from the cream cheese, corn tortillas to give the dish body, and chicken to give it some heart. You'll love how easily these come together.

Packaging: Snack-size zip-top freezer bag, 9 × 13-inch (23 × 33 cm) baking dish with lid

Vegetable oil, for frying tortillas

12 corn tortillas

4 cups (560 g) chopped cooked chicken

2 cups (240 g) shredded pepper jack cheese, divided

8 ounces (224 g) cream cheese, softened

½ cup (80 g) chopped onion

1 teaspoon Chipotle Taco Seasoning Mix (page 30)

Salt and freshly ground black pepper

WHEN READY TO SERVE, YOU WILL NEED:

2 cups (470 ml) salsa verde

—
Serves 4 to 6

Fill a skillet with vegetable oil to a depth of 1 inch (2.5 cm). Heat over medium heat until the oil shimmers. Fry the tortillas in the hot oil for 30 to 45 seconds each, turning once with tongs. Drain the tortillas on paper towels. Allow the tortillas to cool enough to be easily handled.

In a bowl, combine the chicken, 1 cup (120 g) of the jack cheese, the cream cheese, onion, and taco seasoning mix. Season the mixture to taste with salt and pepper.

Place the remaining 1 cup (120 g) of jack cheese in the freezer bag and set aside.

Grease the baking dish.

Assemble the enchiladas by placing 2 tablespoons (28 g) filling on each tortilla. Roll and place the enchiladas, seam side down, in the prepared baking dish.

FREEZING: Place the bag of cheese atop the enchiladas, wrap the dish for the freezer, and chill in the refrigerator before freezing.

TO THAW AND SERVE: Thaw completely in the refrigerator. Remove the bag of jack cheese from the dish. Preheat the oven to 350°F (180°C or gas mark 4). Pour the salsa over the enchiladas and sprinkle the reserved cheese over the enchiladas. Bake the enchiladas for 20 minutes, or until the dish is heated through and the cheese is melted.

Spicy Shrimp and Tomatoes

Succulent shrimp and juicy tomatoes are a great combination in this dish. When you're ready to serve, the seafood cooks quickly in the tangy sauce, making for a speedy weeknight meal. Serve this spicy mixture over hot cooked rice or with cornbread.

Packaging: Two quart-size (1 L) plastic containers with lids

2 tablespoons (30 ml) olive oil

1 cup (150 g) chopped red or green bell pepper, or a combination

1 cup (160 g) chopped onion

1 cup (120 g) chopped celery

1 tablespoon chopped garlic

One 14.5-ounce (406 g) can diced tomatoes, with their juices

One 15-ounce (420 g) can tomato sauce

1 cup (235 ml) water

One 6-ounce (168 g) can tomato paste

1 teaspoon smoked paprika

1 teaspoon dried thyme

1 teaspoon salt

1 teaspoon dried oregano

1 bay leaf

½ teaspoon freshly ground black pepper

½ teaspoon chipotle chile powder

⅛ teaspoon ⅛ crushed red pepper flakes

WHEN READY TO SERVE, YOU WILL NEED:

2 pounds (908 g) shrimp (41 to 50 count), peeled and deveined

—
Serves 6 to 10

In a large stockpot, heat the oil over medium heat until shimmering. Add the peppers, onion, celery, and garlic, and cook until the vegetables are tender and the onions are translucent, about 10 minutes.

Stir in the tomatoes, tomato sauce, water, tomato paste, and seasonings. Bring the mixture to a low boil. Simmer for 20 minutes.

Ladle the sauce into the quart-size (1 L) plastic containers. Allow the sauce to cool to room temperature.

FREEZING: Cover and chill the sauce in the refrigerator before storing in the freezer.

TO THAW AND SERVE: Thaw the sauce and the shrimp (if necessary) in the refrigerator. Heat the sauce in a large saucepan over medium heat. Add the shrimp to the sauce and cook for 3 to 5 minutes, until the shrimp are pink. Adjust the seasonings to taste.

Chipotle Chicken and Onion Wraps

Frozen burritos are great on-the-go food. But this particular version takes "to go" to a whole new level. Filled with a creamy chipotle chicken mixture, these burritos will disappear quickly.

Packaging: Gallon-size (4 L) zip-top freezer bags

1 tablespoon (14 g) salted butter

½ cup (80 g) finely chopped onion

6 cups (840 g) diced cooked chicken

8 ounces (224 g) Neufchâtel cheese, softened

2 tablespoons (18 g) chopped chipotle chile peppers in adobo sauce

1 tablespoon chopped fresh parsley or 1 teaspoon dried parsley flakes

12 burrito-size flour tortillas

—
Serves 6 to 12

In a small sauté pan, melt the butter over medium heat. Add the onion and cook, stirring, until the onion is translucent. Cover the pan and reduce the heat to low. Allow the onion to cook for about 5 minutes more. Remove the lid and stir the onion, continuing to cook until it is very tender and starting to brown.

Combine the chicken, Neufchâtel cheese, cooked onions, chipotle chile and sauce, and parsley in a large bowl. Stir well. (You can combine these ingredients in the bowl of a stand mixer, mixing on low speed just until combined.)

Assemble the wraps by laying each tortilla on a flat surface. Spread a scant ½ cup (70 g) of the chicken filling down the center of each tortilla.

Roll the tortillas up, folding in the sides as you go. Place the wraps in the freezer bag(s).

FREEZING: Seal the wraps in the bag(s), removing as much air as possible. Store in the freezer.

TO THAW AND SERVE: The wraps can be heated directly from the freezer or thawed. Microwave a frozen wrap on a plate for 2 to 3 minutes, turning once. Or thaw the burritos in the refrigerator and then crisp them on a hot griddle until the filling is hot.

CHAPTER 3
Sizzling Pork and Sausage

Southwest Seasoned Pork Chops

These pork chops gain a depth of flavor from the simple marinade and the grill. Pair these chops with fried potatoes, corn, and black beans for a hearty meal. Mix up a batch of Basic Taco Seasoning Mix (page 29) first, as that spice blend plays a starring role in the marinade.

Packaging: Gallon-size (4 L) zip-top freezer bag

¼ cup (60 ml) red wine vinegar

¼ cup (60 ml) vegetable oil

1 tablespoon Basic Taco Seasoning Mix (page 29)

4 boneless pork chops, about ½ inch (1.3 cm) thick

—

Serves 4

Place the freezer bag in a medium bowl, folding the top over the edges. Pour in the vinegar and oil, and add the taco seasoning. Massage the bag to combine the marinade ingredients.

Add the pork chops to the bag. Seal the bag, squeezing out as much air as possible. Massage the bag to distribute the marinade evenly.

FREEZING: Freeze the bag flat in the freezer.

TO THAW AND SERVE: Thaw the chops on a tray or dish in the refrigerator. Grill or broil the thawed pork chops, turning once, until cooked through, 10 to 15 minutes. Serve hot.

Queso Fundido

This meal has been a mainstay in our family for almost twenty years. Delicious and easy to prepare, it's got a little kick, thanks to the spicy cheese and the hot sausage. It's ideal for taking to a potluck or to share with a friend. Serve a green salad, beans, and rice as side dishes. For milder flavor, use mild Italian sausage and Monterey Jack cheese.

Packaging: 8-inch (20.3 cm) pie plate or other 1-quart (1 L) baking dish with lid or foil, gallon-size (4 L) zip-top freezer bag

1 pound (454 g) hot Italian sausage, casings removed

1 cup (160 g) chopped onion

2 cups (240 g) shredded pepper jack cheese

WHEN READY TO SERVE, YOU WILL NEED:

12 corn tortillas or soft taco-size flour tortillas

Sour cream

Easy Homemade Salsa (page 29)

—

Serves 4

In a large skillet, brown the sausage and onion over medium-high heat, breaking up any big chunks of meat with the back of a spoon, for about 10 minutes, or until the meat is just cooked and no longer pink. Drain off any grease.

Grease the pie plate. Spoon the mixture into the pie plate and set aside to cool.

Cover the cooled sausage with the shredded cheese.

FREEZING: Wrap the pie plate in foil and place it inside a zip-top freezer bag. Chill the dish in the refrigerator before freezing.

TO THAW AND SERVE: Thaw the pie plate in the refrigerator. Preheat the oven to 350°F (180°C or gas mark 4). Bake, uncovered, for 15 to 20 minutes, or until the cheese is melted and bubbling. Serve with the tortillas, sour cream, and salsa.

Make-Ahead Baked Bacon

Bacon for the freezer? Really? Yes, really. Having precooked bacon on hand enables you to make a quick BLT or breakfast sandwich. It also helps you prepare in advance for weekend brunches or a houseful of guests. And everything is better with bacon! Grab a few slices whenever you want to add a little smoky crunch to a dish. The easiest way to cook bacon is in the oven, not in a pan on the stove. The mess and time are both greatly reduced. Just watch it carefully to prevent burning.

Packaging: Gallon-size (4 L) zip-top freezer bag

1 pound (454 g) sliced bacon

—
Serves 4

Preheat the oven to 375°F (190°C or gas mark 5). Line a rimmed baking sheet with aluminum foil.

Separate the slices of bacon and lay them on the sheet. Avoid overlapping the slices if possible.

Bake for 15 to 20 minutes, turning the slices over about midway through the cooking time. As oven temperatures and thickness of bacon can vary, check often to prevent burning. Once the bacon is cooked to your desired doneness, remove the pan from the oven.

Drain the bacon on paper towels.

FREEZING: Place the strips of bacon on a foil-lined tray in the freezer and freeze. Once the bacon is frozen, place the slices in the freezer bag. Seal the bag, squeezing out as much air as possible.

TO THAW AND SERVE: Remove the desired number of bacon slices from the freezer bag and reheat in a pan on the stovetop or between paper towels in the microwave until hot. Serve immediately.

Red Sauce with Sausage

This meaty red sauce is simple and delicious. It freezes well and complements pasta dishes beautifully. One of the secrets to its rich flavor is cooking the sausages in the sauce, a trick I owe to a fellow homeschool mom, Carla Luffman. This recipe is an adaptation of one her family has long enjoyed. Feel free to use sweet sausage, spicy sausage, or a mixture. If you are pressed for time, omit the sausages, stir in some beef broth, and reduce the cooking time to 2 hours total.

Packaging: Glass jars or plastic containers with lids, quart-size (1 L) zip-top freezer bags for the sausages

2 tablespoons (30 ml) olive oil

1 cup (160 g) chopped onion

2 cloves garlic, chopped

Four 28-ounce (784 g) cans tomato puree

3 cups (705 ml) water

1 tablespoon (18 g) salt

3 tablespoons chopped fresh Italian parsley or 1 tablespoon dried parsley flakes

3 tablespoons chopped fresh basil or 1 tablespoon dried basil

1½ teaspoons dried oregano

¼ teaspoon red pepper flakes

2 pounds (908 g) Italian sausage links

WHEN READY TO SERVE, YOU WILL NEED:

Cooked pasta

—
Serves 10 to 12

In a large pot, heat the olive oil over medium heat and cook the onion and garlic until softened. Add the tomato puree and water. Stir to mix thoroughly, then add the salt, parsley, basil, oregano, and red pepper flakes.

Cover and simmer for 2 hours, stirring occasionally. Add the sausages and cook, covered, for another 2 hours.

FREEZING: Divide the sausages into meal-size portions in freezer bags. Squeeze out as much air as possible and seal the bags. Pour the sauce into containers. Chill the sausages and the sauce in the refrigerator before storing in the freezer.

TO THAW AND SERVE: Thaw a container of sauce and a bag of sausages in the refrigerator. Reheat them together in a saucepan and serve over pasta.

Versatile Slow-Cooked Carnitas

Carnitas, while translating as "little meats" in Spanish, typically signifies a seasoned, shredded pork filling used for tacos, tostadas, and tamales. Traditionally, the pork shoulder is boiled and then roasted. Here, it is prepared in a slow cooker for a simpler, yet equally delicious result. The moist and juicy carnitas freezes and reheats quite well, making it a perfect addition to your freezer cooking arsenal. Instead of a shoulder roast, you can use country-style pork strips, which often go on sale.

Packaging: Quart-size (1 L) zip-top freezer bags or plastic containers with lids

One 3- to 4-pound (1362 to 1816 g) pork shoulder roast

Salt and freshly ground black pepper

1 medium-size onion, chopped

½ teaspoon dried oregano

¼ cup (60 ml) water

—
Serves 10 to 12

Place the pork roast in a 4-quart (4 L) slow cooker. Season the meat generously with salt and pepper. Add the chopped onion and sprinkle the oregano over all. Add the water to the pot.

Cook on LOW for 8 hours or on HIGH for about 4 hours. The meat should be very tender and shred easily.

Remove the meat from the pot. Strain the juices and reserve them to add to chili, stew, or soup.

Shred and cut the meat into bite-size pieces.

FREEZING: Divide the carnitas into meal-size portions in freezer bags or containers. Chill the meat in the refrigerator before freezing.

TO THAW AND SERVE: Thaw the meat in the refrigerator. Preheat the oven to 350°F (180°C or gas mark 4). Place the meat in a baking dish and reheat for 15 minutes, until hot. Adjust the seasonings to taste.

Pork and Chile Tamales

Tamales are a Christmas tradition in Mexico and southern California. Though I was born and raised in southern California, I did not grow up enjoying homemade tamales. I wish I had! Years ago, my husband suggested that we learn how to make them ourselves. Now, we often keep a few batches of tamales stashed in the freezer. They freeze beautifully and are a delicious snack, lunch, or dinner.

Packaging: Quart- (1 L) or gallon-size (4 L) zip-top freezer bags

(continued)

1 package dried corn husks

1⅓ cups (300 g) unsalted butter, softened

4 cups (480 g) masa harina

2 teaspoons salt

2 to 3 cups (470 to 705 ml) chicken broth

2 cups (280 g) Versatile Slow-Cooked Carnitas (opposite page)

½ to 1 cup (120 to 235 ml) red chile sauce or enchilada sauce

WHEN READY TO SERVE, YOU WILL NEED:

Additional red chile sauce or enchilada sauce

Sour cream

Easy Homemade Salsa (page 29)

—
Serves 12 to 15

Soak the corn husks in warm water until pliable, up to several hours. Remove any silks or debris from the husks and rinse the husks thoroughly. Keep the husks damp until ready to use.

In a large bowl, whip the butter until light and fluffy. Blend in the masa harina, salt, and 2 cups (470 ml) of chicken broth. Blend well. Add more chicken broth until the dough holds together well. It should have the consistency of soft cookie dough. Cover the prepared masa with a damp cloth and keep it cool until ready to use.

In a medium bowl, combine the carnitas and enough of the red chile sauce to moisten it. Taste for seasoning and adjust as desired.

For each tamale, lay a presoaked husk flat on a work surface with the tip away from you. Spread 2 tablespoons (28 g) masa on the husk, in a 5 × 4-inch (12.7 × 10 cm) rectangle. Spoon 2 tablespoons (28 g) carnitas filling in a line down the center of the masa rectangle.

Fold the right side of the corn husk over the center of the filling, then fold the left side over the filling, wrapping any uncovered husk around the tamale. Fold the ends over.

Lay each tamale in a steamer basket, folded side down to hold it shut. Once all the tamales are folded and arranged in the steamer, place the steamer basket in a large pot over a few inches of boiling water. Make sure that the steam can move freely around the tamales; don't pack them in too tightly.

Cover the pot and turn the heat to medium so that the water will boil gently. Steam the tamales for 45 minutes to 1 hour.

To test for doneness, remove one tamale from the top of the stack and one from the middle. Open them; they are done if the masa dough is firm, does not stick to the husk, and does not have a raw, doughy taste.

FREEZING: Cool the tamales completely and package them in freezer bags. Chill in the refrigerator before freezing.

TO SERVE: Steam the frozen tamales for 20 to 30 minutes or until heated through. Or microwave frozen tamales on a plate, covered with a damp paper towel, for 1 to 2 minutes per tamale. Serve the tamales with red chile sauce, sour cream, and salsa.

Cranberry Pork Chops

This meal is ideal for a cold, blustery day. Cranberries, onions, and spices join forces to flavor the pork chops as they simmer in the slow cooker. Prep couldn't be easier, as the meat and seasonings are ready to go in one zip-top freezer bag. Just empty the bag into the cooker, turn it on, and go about your day.

Packaging: Gallon-size (4 L) zip-top freezer bag

2 tablespoons (28 g) salted butter

½ cup (80 g) chopped onion

¼ cup (30 g) chopped celery

1 clove garlic, chopped

1 cup (100 g) fresh cranberries

4 boneless pork chops, about ½ inch (1.3 cm) thick

¼ teaspoon freshly ground black pepper

½ teaspoon dried thyme

2 tablespoons (24 g) brown sugar

WHEN READY TO SERVE, YOU WILL NEED:

¼ cup (60 ml) chicken broth or vegetable broth

—
Serves 4

In a large skillet, melt the butter over medium heat. Add the onion, celery, and garlic, and cook, stirring, until the vegetables are tender. Set the mixture aside to cool completely.

Place the cooled, sautéed vegetables, cranberries, pork chops, pepper, thyme, and brown sugar in the freezer bag.

Seal the bag, squeezing out as much air as possible. Massage the bag to distribute the ingredients evenly.

FREEZING: Freeze the bag flat in the freezer.

TO THAW AND SERVE: Thaw the pork chops on a tray or dish in the refrigerator. On the morning of the day you plan to serve this dish, empty the contents of the bag into a 4-quart (4 L) slow cooker and add ¼ cup (60 ml) broth. Cook on LOW for 6 to 8 hours, or until the pork chops are cooked through.

Shells Stuffed with Pork, Mushrooms, and Onions

These shells have a magical quality. Even the pickiest of eaters will devour them in seconds. I know, because I've watched it happen numerous times. The delicately seasoned pork is mild without being bland. Use a great sauce like Easy Slow Cooker Red Sauce (page 89) for an exceptional meal. And do not overcook the noodles; they will soften further during freezing and baking. For smaller portions, simply divide the shells into smaller baking dishes.

Packaging: 9 × 13-inch (23 × 33 cm) baking dish with lid

12 ounces (340 g) jumbo pasta shells

1¼ pounds (568 g) ground pork

½ cup (80 g) diced onion

1 cup (75 g) finely chopped fresh mushrooms

¼ teaspoon dried oregano

¼ teaspoon dried thyme

Salt and freshly ground black pepper

3 cups (360 g) shredded mozzarella cheese, divided

¼ cup (25 g) freshly grated Parmesan cheese

3 cups (705 ml) Easy Slow Cooker Red Sauce (page 89) or other favorite red sauce

—
Serves 4 to 6

In a large pot of boiling, salted water, cook the shells according to the package directions just until al dente. Drain and set aside to cool.

In a large skillet over medium heat, cook the pork, onion, and mushrooms for about 10 minutes or until the meat is no longer pink. Stir in the oregano and thyme. Season the mixture to taste with salt and pepper. Transfer to a large bowl to cool.

Add 2 cups (240 g) of the mozzarella cheese and the Parmesan cheese to the cooled pork mixture and stir to combine.

Grease the baking dish. Fill the cooled shells with the pork mixture and arrange them in the prepared baking dish. Top the filled shells with the pasta sauce. Sprinkle the shells with the remaining 1 cup (120 g) mozzarella cheese.

FREEZING: Cover and chill the casserole in the refrigerator before freezing.

TO THAW AND SERVE: Thaw the shells in the refrigerator. Preheat the oven to 375°F (190°C or gas mark 5). Bake for 15 to 20 minutes, until hot and bubbly. Serve immediately.

Gingery Pork and Mushroom Lettuce Wraps

You might not expect a meal involving a lettuce wrap to be freezer-friendly. But it can be if you prepare the cooked component first and store it in the freezer. Add the lettuce leaves and other fresh elements right before serving. The ginger-seasoned pork and mushrooms come together quickly and easily for a light summertime supper or elegant appetizer.

Packaging: Quart-size (1 L) zip-top freezer bag or plastic container with lid

1 pound (454 g) ground pork

8 ounces (224 g) fresh mushrooms, finely chopped

2 teaspoons minced fresh ginger

2 cloves garlic, minced

⅛ teaspoon red pepper flakes

1 tablespoon (15 ml) sherry

1 tablespoon (15 ml) soy sauce

1 tablespoon (15 ml) water

1 tablespoon cornstarch

Lettuce leaves

Chopped fresh cilantro

Chopped scallions

Shredded carrots

Asian Dipping Sauce (recipe follows), soy sauce, sriracha sauce, or chili sauce

—
Serves 4

In a large skillet, cook the pork and mushrooms over medium-high heat until the pork is cooked through and the mushrooms start to brown slightly, about 10 minutes.

Stir in the ginger, garlic, and red pepper.

In a small bowl, combine the sherry, soy sauce, water, and cornstarch. Add the sauce to the skillet and cook, stirring, until the sauce thickens.

FREEZING: Cool the pork mixture to room temperature. Spoon the mixture into a freezer bag or plastic container. Chill the mixture in the refrigerator before freezing.

TO THAW AND SERVE: Thaw the pork mixture in the refrigerator. Reheat the mixture in a large skillet or in the microwave. Spoon several spoonfuls of the pork mixture into each lettuce leaf. Top with cilantro, scallion, and carrot. Serve with the sauce of your choice.

Asian Dipping Sauce

This recipe from my friend Jessika also makes a great dipping sauce for pot stickers or spring rolls.

⅓ cup (80 ml) soy sauce

¼ cup (60 ml) rice vinegar

3 cloves garlic, minced

2 tablespoons (30 ml) sesame oil

2 tablespoons (25 g) sugar

1 tablespoon minced fresh ginger

¼ teaspoon freshly ground black pepper

¼ teaspoon crushed red pepper flakes

—
Makes about 1 cup (235 ml)

Combine all of the ingredients in a glass bowl and microwave until warmed through. Alternatively, heat the sauce over low heat in a small saucepan.

Herbed Pork Sausage Patties

Want a change of pace from your regular burger? Looking for a spicy accompaniment to your eggs in the morning? How about a simple homemade sausage? You can't go wrong with this version, which mixes up quickly and freezes beautifully. Store the patties, cooked or uncooked, in the freezer for quick breakfast or lunch fare.

Packaging: Waxed paper, plastic wrap, gallon-size (4 L) zip-top freezer bag

1 pound (454 g) lean ground pork

2 tablespoons (28 g) salted butter, softened

2 cloves garlic, chopped

1 teaspoon salt

½ teaspoon onion powder

¼ teaspoon freshly ground black pepper

¼ teaspoon rubbed sage

⅛ teaspoon dried thyme

⅛ teaspoon paprika

⅛ teaspoon cayenne pepper

⅛ teaspoon dry mustard

—

Serves 6

In the bowl of a stand mixer, mix all of the ingredients until the mixture is well blended and starts to bind together.

With wet hands, divide the pork mixture into six equal portions. Pat each portion into a flat patty.

FREEZING: If freezing uncooked, stack the patties with a square of waxed paper between each one. Wrap the stack in plastic wrap and place in a freezer bag.

If freezing precooked, preheat the oven to 400°F (200°C or gas mark 6) and cook the patties on a foil-lined rimmed baking sheet, flipping once, for 10 to 15 minutes, or until cooked through. Drain the cooked patties on paper towels. Cool completely. Freeze the patties on a tray, and then transfer to a freezer bag. Seal the bag, squeezing out as much air as possible. Return the patties to the freezer.

TO THAW AND SERVE: For uncooked patties, thaw in the refrigerator. Preheat the oven to 400°F (200°C or gas mark 6). Bake the unwrapped patties on a foil-lined rimmed baking sheet, flipping once, for 10 to 15 minutes, or until cooked through.

For cooked patties, thaw in the refrigerator. Preheat the oven to 400°F (200°C or gas mark 6). Reheat the patties 5 to 10 minutes, or until heated through. You can also reheat them without thawing; add about 5 minutes to the oven time.

Zesty Italian Melts

My husband's favorite sandwich features Italian meats and herbed mayonnaise on a roll, which we often eat cold and freshly made. I've transformed it here into a freezer-friendly sub that's baked or grilled before serving, resulting in hot, melty, meaty goodness. Serve this one with a salad or a cup of vegetable soup.

Packaging: Heavy-duty aluminum foil, 3 to 4 gallon-size (3 to 4 L) zip-top freezer bags

½ cup (112 g) (1 stick) unsalted butter, softened

2 teaspoons chopped fresh basil or ½ teaspoon dried basil

1 teaspoon minced garlic

¼ teaspoon dried oregano

8 Italian rolls, sliced lengthwise, with one long edge attached

8 slices ham

24 slices salami

8 slices mozzarella cheese

—

Serves 8

In a small bowl, combine the softened butter, basil, garlic, and oregano. Blend well. Spread a thin layer of the garlic butter on each roll.

Layer one slice of ham, three slices of salami, and one slice of cheese on each roll. Close the rolls and wrap each tightly with aluminum foil.

FREEZING: Place all the wrapped rolls in the freezer bags. Store the sandwiches in the freezer.

TO THAW AND SERVE: Thaw the desired number of sandwiches in the refrigerator. Preheat the oven to 325°F (170°C or gas mark 3). Bake the wrapped sandwiches for 15 to 25 minutes, or until the bread is crusty and the cheese is melted. Alternatively, you can cook the thawed sandwiches in a panini press until hot.

CHAPTER 4
Meatless Marvels

Bean and Cheese Nacho Bake

This versatile bean and cheese casserole can be served as a main dish, accompanied by salad and rice, or as an appetizer with chips. Using homemade salsa will give it a fresher taste.

Packaging: 9 × 13-inch (23 × 33 cm) baking dish with lid

3 cups (750 g) canned refried beans

⅓ cup (53 g) finely chopped onion

1 teaspoon chopped garlic

1 cup (235 ml) Easy Homemade Salsa (page 29) or other favorite salsa

⅔ cup (65 g) canned sliced black olives, drained

1 cup (235 ml) tomato sauce

2 cups (240 g) shredded pepper jack cheese, divided

1 cup (225 g) ricotta cheese

⅔ cup (155 g) sour cream

½ teaspoon ground cumin

6½ ounces (182 g) crushed tortilla chips (about 3 cups)

—
Serves 6 to 8

Grease the baking dish.

In a large bowl, combine the beans, onion, garlic, salsa, black olives, and tomato sauce.

In another bowl, combine 1 cup (120 g) of the jack cheese, the ricotta, sour cream, and cumin.

Place half of the chips in the bottom of the baking dish, spreading to cover. Spread half of the bean mixture over the chips. Spread all of the cheese mixture over the bean layer. Repeat the layers, using the remaining chips, bean mixture, and remaining 1 cup (120 g) jack cheese.

FREEZING: Cover and chill in the refrigerator before freezing.

TO THAW AND SERVE: Thaw the casserole in the refrigerator. Preheat the oven to 350°F (180°C or gas mark 4). Bake for 40 minutes, or until the casserole is hot and the cheese is bubbly.

Quick and Easy Cheese Enchiladas

Imagine delicious Mexican fare for supper—without having to wait hours for a table. This meal is it! Partnered with rice and beans and a green salad, cheese enchiladas make an ideal meatless meal. This recipe yields two large pans of a dozen enchiladas each. But you can package them in whatever size baking dishes best suit the number of people you're serving.

Packaging: Two 9 × 13-inch (23 × 33 cm) baking dishes with lids

Vegetable oil, for frying

24 corn tortillas

4 cups (480 g) shredded cheddar and/or Monterey Jack cheese, divided

One 28-ounce (784 g) can red enchilada sauce

One 2.25-ounce (63 g) can sliced black olives

¼ cup (25 g) sliced scallions

—
Serves 8 to 12

Fill a skillet with vegetable oil to a depth of 1 inch (2.5 cm). Heat over medium heat until the oil shimmers. Fry the tortillas in the hot oil until the texture is a bit leathery but not crisp, 20 to 30 seconds, turning once. Drain the tortillas on paper towels and set aside until cool enough to handle.

Grease the baking dishes.

Set aside 1 cup (120 g) of cheese. For each enchilada, place a small handful of cheese down the center of each tortilla, roll up, and place, seam side down, in a greased baking dish. Continue until all the tortillas are rolled and the baking dishes are filled. You should be able to fit 12 enchiladas in each dish.

Pour the enchilada sauce over the tops of the rolled tortillas. Sprinkle the reserved 1 cup (120 g) cheese as well as the olives and scallions over the top.

FREEZING: Cover the enchiladas and chill in the refrigerator before freezing.

TO THAW AND SERVE: Thaw the enchiladas in the refrigerator. Preheat the oven to 350°F (180°C or gas mark 4). Bake the enchiladas until they are heated through and the cheese is melted, about 15 minutes. You can also bake this directly from the freezer; allow an extra 15 to 30 minutes of baking time.

Cozy Cheese and Potato Casserole

At first glance, you might confuse this delectable concoction of potatoes and cheese with the "church potatoes" or hash brown casseroles of yore. However, unlike its predecessors, this potato bake features a homemade cream of celery soup that puts the canned version to shame. It's important to use frozen potatoes in this dish; uncooked fresh potatoes will blacken in the freezer. Commercially frozen hash brown potatoes work exceptionally well here. Don't let them thaw as you mix up this casserole. Stir it up quickly, spoon it into the pan, and pop it into the freezer.

Packaging: 9 × 13-inch (23 × 33 cm) baking dish with lid

2 cups (470 ml) Homemade Cream of Celery Soup for Cooking (page 93), chilled

1½ cups (180 g) shredded cheddar cheese

1 cup (225 g) sour cream

1 teaspoon kosher salt

¼ teaspoon freshly ground black pepper

One 32-ounce (908 g) bag frozen shredded potatoes

1 teaspoon paprika

—
Serves 6 to 8

Grease the baking dish.

In a large bowl, combine the celery soup, cheese, sour cream, salt, and pepper. Stir in the frozen shredded potatoes, combining well.

Spoon the potato mixture into the prepared dish. Sprinkle the paprika over the top.

FREEZING: Cover and freeze.

TO THAW AND SERVE: Thaw the casserole in the refrigerator. Preheat the oven to 375°F (190°C or gas mark 5). Bake the casserole for about 1 hour, or until it is heated through and the cheese is melted.

Green Chile Rice Casserole

Rice, cheese, and chiles combine in a comfort-food dish that will disappear quickly. Brown rice boasts a denser texture and a nuttier flavor than white rice. It also holds up better in the freezer, making it the perfect base for this rich and creamy casserole. You will want to cook the rice ahead of time so that it can cool before you assemble the casserole. Sour cream adds great flavor, but Greek yogurt has it beat with less fat and extra protein.

Packaging: 8-inch (20.3 cm) square baking dish or 3-quart (3 L) baking dish with lid

3 cups (510 g) cooked brown rice, at room temperature

16 ounces (454 g) plain Greek-style yogurt or sour cream

2 cups (240 g) shredded cheddar cheese

One 4-ounce (112 g) can chopped green chiles

1 tablespoon finely chopped jalapeño peppers

¼ teaspoon ground cumin

⅛ teaspoon freshly ground black pepper

—
Serves 4 to 6

Grease the baking dish. Combine all of the ingredients in a large bowl. Spoon the mixture into the prepared pan.

FREEZING: Cover and chill in the refrigerator before freezing.

TO THAW AND SERVE: Thaw the dish in the refrigerator. Preheat the oven to 350°F (180°C or gas mark 4). Bake the casserole for 25 to 40 minutes, or until heated through.

Pepper Jack and Chile Burritos

Frozen burritos make quick snacks or main dishes. After an overnight thaw in the refrigerator, these will crisp perfectly on a hot griddle, for a healthier alternative to chimichangas. Top with enchilada sauce, shredded lettuce, tomatoes, and sour cream. For even quicker eats, simply microwave the frozen burritos for a minute or two. To prevent the burritos from cracking when you roll them, use fresh tortillas that are at room temperature.

Packaging: Gallon-size (4 L) zip-top freezer bags, aluminum foil or plastic wrap (optional)

4 cups (1000 g) canned refried beans

2 cups (240 g) shredded pepper jack cheese

One 4-ounce (112 g) can chopped green chiles

12 burrito-size flour tortillas

—
Serves 6 to 12

In a large bowl, combine the beans, cheese, and green chiles.

Fill the burritos by spooning a scant ½ cup (125 g) of the filling down the center of each tortilla. Roll it up, tucking in the sides as you go. As each burrito is rolled, place it in a freezer bag. If you like, you can wrap each burrito in aluminum foil or plastic wrap before placing it in the freezer bag.

FREEZING: Seal the burritos in the bags, squeezing out as much air as possible. Store the bags of burritos in the freezer.

TO THAW AND SERVE: Thaw as many burritos as desired in the refrigerator.

TO REHEAT IN THE MICROWAVE: Cook thawed burritos, flipping once, 1 to 2 minutes per burrito, or until hot. You can also reheat them directly from the freezer, without thawing; just add an additional minute or two of cooking time.

TO REHEAT ON THE GRIDDLE: Cook thawed burritos on a hot griddle until the filling is hot and the tortilla is crisp.

TO REHEAT IN THE OVEN: Preheat the oven to 350°F (180°C or gas mark 4). For crispy burritos, bake thawed burritos for 15 to 20 minutes. For softer burritos, wrap each in foil prior to baking. If the burritos are frozen, increase the cooking time by 5 to 10 minutes.

Easy Stovetop Ratatouille

A traditional French vegetable stew, ratatouille is summer captured in a bowl. There is great debate over the proper preparation of ratatouille—vegetables cooked together or separately? This simple version is mixed in one pot and simmered on the stovetop. A vegan dish that is good served hot or even at room temperature, it's a delicious way to preserve the bounty of the summer garden. Provide lots of sliced baguette for soaking up the juices. Avoid overcooking the vegetables, so that they are not soggy when reheated.

Packaging: Plastic containers with lids

¼ cup (60 ml) olive oil

1 cup (160 g) chopped onion

1 tablespoon chopped garlic

1 red bell pepper, chopped

1 green bell pepper, chopped

1 medium zucchini, sliced into ¼-inch (6 mm)-thick half-moons

1 small yellow squash, sliced

1 eggplant, peeled and cubed

4 ounces (112 g) fresh mushrooms, sliced

Two 14.5-ounce (406 g) cans petite diced tomatoes with juices

1½ teaspoons *herbes de Provence*

1 teaspoon kosher salt

—
Serves 6 to 8

In a large heavy pot, heat the oil over medium heat until shimmering. Add the onion and garlic, and cook until the onions are translucent.

Add the peppers, zucchini, yellow squash, eggplant, and mushrooms, and sauté for about 5 minutes, stirring occasionally.

Add the tomatoes, *herbes de Provence*, and salt. Stir to combine. Cook for about 30 minutes, or until the vegetables are just tender.

FREEZING: Divide the ratatouille into meal-size portions in plastic containers and chill in the refrigerator before freezing.

TO THAW AND SERVE: Thaw the ratatouille in the refrigerator. Reheat in a saucepan. Serve hot, warm, or at room temperature.

Broccoli Gratin with Tarragon and Buttered Bread Crumbs

This creamy broccoli-and-cheese casserole makes a delicious meatless main dish when accompanied by a salad and bread. Homemade cream of celery soup replaces the canned variety often seen in traditional casseroles.

Packaging: 9 × 13-inch (23 × 33 cm) baking dish with lid

1½ pounds (680 g) broccoli florets (about 9 cups)

2 cups (470 ml) Homemade Cream of Celery Soup for Cooking (page 93)

½ teaspoon dried tarragon

1 cup (120 g) shredded cheddar cheese, divided

1 cup (50 g) fresh bread crumbs

2 tablespoons (28 g) salted butter, melted

—
Serves 4 to 6

Grease the baking dish. Steam the broccoli florets until crisp-tender, 8 to 10 minutes.

In a large bowl, combine the broccoli, cream of celery soup, tarragon, and ½ cup (60 g) of the cheddar cheese. Stir gently to combine. Spread the mixture in the bottom of the prepared baking dish. Sprinkle the remaining ½ cup (60 g) cheddar cheese over the top.

In a small bowl, combine the bread crumbs and melted butter. Sprinkle this over the cheese layer.

FREEZING: Cover and chill in the refrigerator before freezing.

TO THAW AND SERVE: Thaw the dish in the refrigerator. Preheat the oven to 350°F (180°C or gas mark 4). Bake the gratin for 30 to 45 minutes, or until hot and bubbly.

Individual Greek Egg Casseroles

In my husband's hometown, there used to be a delightful family owned Greek restaurant where we often ate as newlyweds. One of my favorite meals at Pavlako's was the Greek eggs, which featured the delicious combination of spinach and feta. I've re-created Pavlako's Greek eggs in this individual egg casserole, which makes a delicious lunch or dinner when served with a side salad and a roll. Make several individual casseroles at one time by multiplying the recipe, lining up all the dishes and ingredients, and preparing them assembly-line style.

Packaging: 2-cup (470 ml) baking dish with lid

1 cup (50 g) soft bread cubes from an Italian loaf

⅓ cup (40 g) crumbled feta cheese

¼ cup chopped frozen spinach, thawed and squeezed dry

2 large eggs, beaten

½ cup (120 ml) milk

Pinch of freshly ground black pepper

—

Serves 1

Grease the baking dish. Spread the bread cubes across the bottom of the dish. Sprinkle the feta cheese and spinach over the bread cubes.

In a small bowl, whisk together the eggs, milk, and black pepper. Pour the egg mixture over the bread and cheese.

FREEZING: Cover and freeze.

TO THAW AND SERVE: Thaw the casserole in the refrigerator. Preheat the oven to 350°F (180°C or gas mark 4). Bake the casserole for 25 minutes or until the top is puffy and a tester inserted in the center comes out clean. Alternatively, bake directly from the freezer for 40 to 45 minutes.

Tahini Vegetable Patties

These veggie patties combine the flavors of falafel and fresh vegetables, making for a delicious and filling dish. Serve them with Greek yogurt, chopped fresh cilantro, and crumbled feta cheese, or stuff them into pita breads, if you like. Make smaller patties to serve as appetizers.

Packaging: Waxed paper, quart-size (1 L) zip-top freezer bag

1 tablespoon (15 ml) olive oil

½ cup (60 g) shredded zucchini

½ cup (75 g) chopped red bell pepper

½ cup (80 g) chopped onion

1 tablespoon finely chopped jalapeño pepper

1 teaspoon chopped garlic

One 15-ounce (420 g) can garbanzo beans, drained

1¾ cups (85 g) fresh bread crumbs

2 large eggs, beaten

2 tablespoons (28 g) tahini

1 teaspoon kosher salt

WHEN READY TO SERVE, YOU WILL NEED:

Olive oil, for frying

Plain Greek-style yogurt

Chopped fresh cilantro

Crumbled feta cheese

—

Serves 4

In a large skillet over medium-high heat, heat the olive oil. Sauté the zucchini, bell pepper, onion, jalapeño, and garlic. Cook the mixture until the vegetables are tender, about 7 minutes. Remove from the heat and set aside to cool.

In the bowl of a food processor, pulse the garbanzo beans until coarsely chopped. Alternatively, you can mash them with a potato masher.

In a large bowl, combine the sautéed vegetables, garbanzo beans, bread crumbs, eggs, tahini, and salt. Stir gently to combine. Form the mixture into 4 patties.

FREEZING: Stack the patties with a square of waxed paper between each one. Place in a freezer bag and freeze.

TO THAW AND SERVE: Thaw the patties in the refrigerator. Heat 1 to 2 tablespoons (15 to 30 ml) olive oil in a skillet and fry the patties in the hot oil until hot and browned. Serve with the yogurt, cilantro, and feta for toppings.

Tomato Sauce with Oregano and Kalamata Olives

This Mediterranean-style sauce is delicious served over pasta, as a dipping sauce for bread, or even on pizza. It also makes a delicious topping for the Spinach and Feta Manicotti with Lemon and Oregano (page 94).

Packaging: Plastic containers with lids

2 tablespoons (30 ml) olive oil

½ cup (80 g) chopped onion

1 teaspoon chopped garlic

¼ cup (60 ml) white wine

Two 14.5-ounce (406 g) cans petite diced tomatoes with juices

One 15-ounce (420 g) can tomato sauce

⅓ cup (35 g) chopped kalamata olives

2 teaspoons dried oregano

⅛ teaspoon freshly ground black pepper

—
Makes about 6 cups (1410 ml)

In a large stockpot, heat the olive oil over medium heat until shimmering. Add the onion and garlic, and cook, stirring, until the onion becomes translucent, about 5 minutes.

Add the white wine and stir, scraping up any brown bits. Add the diced tomatoes, tomato sauce, olives, oregano, and black pepper. Simmer the mixture for 30 minutes. Taste and adjust the seasonings.

FREEZING: Divide the sauce into meal-size portions in plastic containers. Chill in the refrigerator before freezing.

TO THAW AND SERVE: Thaw the sauce in the refrigerator. Reheat in a saucepan on the stovetop or in a microwave-safe dish in the microwave.

Easy Slow Cooker Red Sauce

When my family needed to economize years ago, I started making my own pasta sauce, and I haven't looked back. About once a month I cook up a big batch, divide it into 2-cup (470 ml) portions, and freeze it. I never buy jarred sauce; we enjoy the homemade version so much more. Serve this sauce over your favorite noodles, or use it in lasagna and other casseroles.

Packaging: Plastic containers with lids

¼ cup (60 ml) olive oil

2 large onions, diced

1 tablespoon chopped garlic

Four 28-ounce (784 g) cans crushed tomatoes

1 to 2 cups (235 to 470 ml) water

1 tablespoon (18 g) salt

⅓ cup (16 g) chopped fresh basil or 2 tablespoons dried basil

3 tablespoons chopped fresh parsley or 1 tablespoon dried parsley flakes

½ teaspoon red pepper flakes

—
Makes 14 to 16 cups (3290 to 3760 ml)

In a large skillet, heat the olive oil over medium heat. Add the onions and garlic and cook until softened. Spoon the onion mixture into a 5-quart (5 L) or larger slow cooker. Add the crushed tomatoes, water, salt, basil, parsley, and red pepper flakes. Cover and cook on low for at least 4 hours. Adjust the seasonings to taste.

FREEZING: Divide the sauce into meal-size portions in plastic containers. Chill in the refrigerator before freezing.

TO THAW AND SERVE: Thaw the sauce in the refrigerator. Reheat in a saucepan over low heat, whisking to recombine.

Sun-Dried Tomato Pesto

Sun-dried tomatoes create a vibrant pesto that works beautifully on pizza, hot pasta, and pasta salads; you can mix it into hamburgers or use it as a topping for chicken breasts. A little goes a long way in adding sunny summer flavor.

Packaging: Plastic containers with lids or pint-size (470 ml) zip-top freezer bags

2 cups (110 g) sun-dried tomatoes

1 cup (100 g) freshly grated Parmesan cheese

¾ cup (90 g) walnuts or pine nuts

3 tablespoons chopped fresh basil or 1 tablespoon dried basil

1 tablespoon chopped garlic

1 teaspoon freshly ground black pepper

¼ teaspoon red pepper flakes

¾ cup (180 ml) olive oil

—

Makes 2½ cups (590 g)

In a food processor fitted with a metal blade, combine the sun-dried tomatoes, cheese, nuts, basil, garlic, black pepper, and red pepper flakes. Process until smooth.

With the machine running, pour in the olive oil in a slow stream. Process until combined.

FREEZING: Divide into ½-cup (120 ml) portions in plastic containers or pint-size (470 ml) zip-top freezer bags and chill in the refrigerator before freezing.

TO THAW AND SERVE: Thaw in the refrigerator. Stir to recombine the ingredients before using.

Roasted Vegetable Soup

I'm pretty sure that you could make a different kind of soup every day of the year and not repeat yourself. There are just so many options—smooth, chunky, noodle, vegetable, chicken—the choices are endless. I love the rich flavors that roasted vegetables bring to this blended soup. While you may not be in the mood for eating soup in the summer when these veggies are at their peak, your Fall Weather Self will thank you that you filled the freezer when you could.

Packaging: Plastic containers with lids

1 eggplant, trimmed and split lengthwise

1 large patty pan squash or 2 yellow squash, trimmed and split in half

2 ribs celery, trimmed

2 bell peppers, seeded and halved

1 cup (120 g) baby carrots or 2 large carrots, peeled and cut into 2-inch (5 cm) chunks

1 cup (150 g) cherry tomatoes or 2 medium tomatoes, halved

4 large cloves garlic, unpeeled

2 tablespoons (30 ml) olive oil

1 tablespoon chopped fresh oregano or 1 teaspoon dried oregano

1 bay leaf

3 to 5 cups (705 to 1175 ml) vegetable or chicken broth

Fine sea salt and freshly ground black pepper

—
Serves 4

Preheat the oven to 400°F (200°C or gas mark 6). Place the vegetables on a rimmed baking sheet. Brush the vegetables with the oil.

Roast the vegetables for 45 minutes, until tender and spotted with brown.

Scoop the eggplant pulp from the skin and place it in a large stockpot. Remove the garlic from its skins and add to the pot as well as the other vegetables, oregano, and bay leaf.

Add 3 cups (705 ml) of the broth and bring to a simmer. Simmer the mixture for about 45 minutes, or until the vegetables are very tender.

Remove the bay leaf and discard. Use an immersion blender to blend the vegetables until smooth. (You can also blend the soup in a blender or in a food processor.) Thin with more stock, if desired. Season to taste with salt and pepper.

FREEZING: Divide the soup into meal-size portions in plastic containers. Chill in the refrigerator before freezing.

TO THAW AND SERVE: Thaw the soup in the refrigerator. Reheat in a saucepan until heated through, stirring to recombine.

Black Bean Soup with Jalapeño

Some black bean soups are laden with bacon. While bacon is certainly not a bad thing, this soup is different in that the flavor of vegetables and beans shines through. Serve it with crusty bread and cheddar cheese or a dollop of sour cream. The soup can be prepared with dried beans, but for quicker cooking, use canned black beans.

Packaging: Plastic containers with lids

1 pound (454 g) dried black beans, rinsed, picked over, and soaked according to package directions, then drained, or four 15-ounce (420 g) cans black beans, rinsed and drained

6 cups (1410 ml) reduced-sodium chicken broth or vegetable broth

1 tablespoon (15 ml) olive oil

1 cup (120 g) shredded carrot

1 cup (160 g) chopped onion

1 cup (120 g) chopped celery

1 tablespoon finely chopped jalapeño pepper

1 teaspoon chopped garlic

1 cup (120 g) shredded potato

1 bay leaf

1 to 2 teaspoons kosher salt

1 teaspoon dried oregano

½ teaspoon ground cumin

¼ teaspoon freshly ground black pepper

1 tablespoon (15 ml) freshly squeezed lemon juice or lime juice

—
Serves 6 to 8

In a large stockpot, combine the soaked dried beans and broth. Bring to a boil and simmer for 2 hours, or until the beans are tender. If you're using canned beans, simply combine the beans and broth and move on to the next step.

In a large heavy skillet, heat the oil over medium heat until shimmering. Sauté the carrot, onion, celery, jalapeño, and garlic until crisp-tender, about 5 minutes.

Transfer the sautéed vegetables to the pot along with the shredded potato, bay leaf, salt, oregano, cumin, and pepper. Stir well and simmer for 1 hour.

Remove the bay leaf and discard it. Stir in the lemon juice. This is a chunky soup. If you prefer it smoother, puree the soup with an immersion blender or in a food processor or blender, in batches if necessary. Adjust the seasonings to taste.

FREEZING: Divide the soup into meal-size portions in plastic containers. Chill in the refrigerator before freezing.

TO THAW AND SERVE: Thaw the soup in the refrigerator. Reheat in a saucepan until heated through, stirring to recombine.

Homemade Cream of Celery Soup for Cooking

Canned cream soup has been a resource for busy home cooks for more than 50 years. However, a quick glance at the label tells us that there might be better foods to feed our bodies. Cook up a bulk batch of this vegetarian cream of celery soup to use in cooking instead. For a richer flavor, use chicken broth or vegetable broth instead of water.

Packaging: Plastic container with lid

¼ cup (56 g) (½ stick) salted butter

¼ cup (30 g) unbleached all-purpose flour

1 cup (235 ml) milk

1 cup (235 ml) water

2 tablespoons (16 g) chopped celery

1 tablespoon freshly grated Parmesan cheese

1 teaspoon salt

¼ teaspoon freshly ground black pepper

¼ teaspoon onion powder

⅛ teaspoon paprika

—
Makes about 2 cups (470 ml)

In a large stockpot, melt the butter over medium heat. Stir in the flour and cook until the mixture bubbles. Cook for 1 more minute, stirring.

Whisk in the milk and water, stirring constantly, until the mixture thickens to a sauce-like consistency.

Stir in the celery, Parmesan cheese, salt, black pepper, onion powder, and paprika. Simmer for 5 minutes.

FREEZING: If using the soup in a recipe, cool it completely and proceed with the recipe. Otherwise, transfer the soup to a plastic container. Chill the soup in the refrigerator before freezing.

TO THAW AND SERVE: Thaw the soup in the refrigerator. Use as directed in recipes.

> **NOTE:**
>
> To make a big batch of this soup, simply multiply all the ingredients by four. The cooking method remains the same.

Spinach and Feta Manicotti with Lemon and Oregano

Spinach and feta cheese are happy companions in a number of Greek dishes. But they steal the show in this easy baked pasta dish. Remember to cook the noodles just until al dente or a tad firmer. The noodles will soften upon freezing and with further baking in the oven. And, if you like, package them in smaller baking dishes or store them in freezer bags without the sauce (freeze the sauce separately). That way, you can bake whatever quantity you want at serving time.

Packaging: 9 × 13-inch (23 × 33 cm) baking dish with lid

1 package manicotti (about 14 manicotti)

One 16-ounce (454 g) package frozen chopped spinach, thawed and
squeezed dry

2 cups (240 g) shredded mozzarella cheese, divided

2 cups (450 g) ricotta cheese

1 cup (120 g) crumbled feta cheese

1 large egg, beaten

Grated zest of 1 lemon

¼ teaspoon dried oregano

3 to 4 cups (705 to 940 ml) Tomato Sauce with Oregano and Kalamata Olives (page 88) or other favorite red sauce

—

Serves 5 to 7

Grease the baking dish.

Cook the manicotti just until al dente, according to the package directions. Drain the noodles.

In a large bowl, combine the spinach, 1 cup (120 g) of the mozzarella cheese, the ricotta, feta cheese, egg, lemon zest, and oregano. Stir well to combine.

Fill the cooked manicotti by spooning a heaping tablespoon of the mixture into each one. You can also fill the manicotti using a piping bag made out of a quart-size (1 L) freezer bag. Spoon the cheese filling into the bag and seal. Snip off one corner of the bag and pipe the filling into the cooked manicotti.

Arrange the manicotti in the prepared baking dish. Pour the sauce over the manicotti. Sprinkle the remaining 1 cup (120 g) mozzarella cheese over the sauce.

FREEZING: Cover and chill the pan in the refrigerator before freezing.

TO THAW AND SERVE: Thaw the manicotti in the refrigerator. Preheat the oven to 350°F (180°C or gas mark 4). Bake the pasta until heated through, about 30 minutes.

Cheesy Butternut Squash Soup with Herbs

Believe it or not, I had never eaten butternut squash until our CSA provided an abundance of them one fall. We are fast friends now. The squash plays so nicely with cheddar in this soup. Happiness in a spoon! I like to package it in single servings for quick lunches on the go.

Packaging: Plastic containers with lids

5 tablespoons (70 g) salted butter, divided

One 2-pound (908 g) butternut squash, peeled, seeded, and cubed, or two 12-ounce (340 g) packages cubed squash

1½ cups (270 g) chopped onion

1 cup (120 g) chopped celery

1 cup (120 g) chopped carrot

1 cup (120 g) diced potato

5 cups (1175 ml) reduced-sodium chicken broth or water

¼ teaspoon rubbed sage

¼ teaspoon dried thyme

⅛ teaspoon dried marjoram

¼ cup (30 g) unbleached all-purpose flour

2 cups (470 ml) milk

2 cups (240 g) shredded cheddar cheese

Salt and freshly ground black pepper

—
Serves 6 to 8

In a large stockpot, melt 3 tablespoons (42 g) of the butter over medium heat. Add the butternut squash and onion. Cook for about 5 minutes, stirring occasionally.

Add the celery, carrot, and potato. Cook 5 minutes more, stirring occasionally.

Add the chicken broth, sage, thyme, and marjoram, and bring to a boil. Reduce the heat and simmer until the vegetables are tender, about 30 minutes.

Meanwhile, melt the remaining 2 tablespoons (28 g) butter in a large pot over medium heat. Whisk in the flour and cook for a minute or two. Whisk in the milk until smooth. Simmer until thickened. Whisk in the cheddar cheese gradually, stirring to incorporate. Remove from the heat.

Puree the vegetable mixture with an immersion blender or in a food processor, in batches if necessary. Stir in the cheese mixture. Season with salt and pepper to taste.

FREEZING: Divide the soup into meal-size portions in plastic containers. Chill in the refrigerator before freezing.

TO THAW AND SERVE: Thaw the soup in the refrigerator. Reheat in a saucepan until heated through.

CHAPTER 5
Breakfasts for Champions

Cranberry-Orange Granola

This granola makes a beautiful gift at the holidays, as well as a fantastic breakfast any time of year. Store the cranberries separately from the granola until you're ready to serve it, so they retain their tenderness and moisture.

Packaging: Plastic containers with lids or gallon-size (4 L) zip-top freezer bag

5 cups (400 g) old-fashioned rolled oats (do not use quick-cooking oats)

1 cup (140 g) chopped nuts, such as walnuts or pecans

1 cup (225 g) light brown sugar

½ cup (120 ml) vegetable oil

½ cup (60 g) powdered nonfat milk, optional

¼ cup (60 ml) water

1 tablespoon ground cinnamon

Grated zest of 1 orange

1 teaspoon vanilla extract

½ teaspoon salt

WHEN READY TO SERVE, YOU WILL NEED:

1 cup (150 g) dried cranberries

—
Serves 6 to 8

Preheat the oven to 300°F (150°C or gas mark 2). Grease a large rimmed baking sheet or line it with parchment paper.

In a large bowl, combine the oats and nuts.

In a medium saucepan over low heat, combine the brown sugar, oil, powdered milk (if using), water, cinnamon, orange zest, vanilla, and salt. Heat, stirring, until just simmering. Pour this mixture over the oats and nuts, stirring to combine.

Spread the mixture on the prepared baking sheet. Bake for 40 to 45 minutes, stirring every 10 to 15 minutes. Cool completely.

FREEZING: Store in a plastic container or freezer bag in the freezer.

TO THAW AND SERVE: Thaw the granola in its container on the counter. Add the cranberries right before serving.

Better Instant Oatmeal Packets

I love breakfast in a box! It makes our mornings go so much more smoothly when I serve food that is easy to prepare and clean up. Even the little kids can do it all by themselves! Cold cereal and instant oatmeal are favorites, but since my children can eat through one box of instant oatmeal packets in a single morning, I've learned to make my own, inspired by a recipe on an archived blog called The Simple Dollar. It takes just minutes to assemble a few dozen packets. I store the packets in a bin the pantry, but you can freeze them for longer storage. To reduce waste, save the empty snack-size bags to refill next month or next week.

Packaging: Snack-size zip-top bag

¼ cup (20 g) quick-cooking rolled oats

1½ teaspoons brown sugar

1 tablespoon raisins, dried cranberries, or dried blueberries (optional)

1 teaspoon powdered nonfat milk (optional)

⅛ teaspoon salt

—
Serves 1

Place the oats, brown sugar, fruit (if using), milk (if using), and salt in the bag. Shake gently to combine. Repeat to make as many additional servings as desired.

FREEZING: Store the bags in the freezer.

TO SERVE: Empty the contents of one bag into a heatproof bowl. Add ¼ to ½ cup (60 to 120 ml) boiling water. If you omitted the milk powder, you can use hot milk instead of boiling water. Let sit for 1 to 2 minutes, then stir before serving.

Spiced Whole-Grain Waffles

These spiced waffles are packed with whole grains and have so much flavor that you can eat them out of hand, without any toppings. My mother, however, says they beg for a scoop of vanilla ice cream. If you decide to package the recipe as a mix, be sure to mark the bag with a list of the wet ingredients to add right before cooking, as well as the cooking instructions.

Packaging: Gallon-size (4 L) zip-top freezer bag

DRY INGREDIENTS:

3½ cups (420 g) unbleached all-purpose flour

2 cups (240 g) whole-wheat pastry flour

¼ cup (20 g) quick-cooking oats

¼ cup (30 g) cornmeal

¼ cup (56 g) dark brown sugar

¼ cup (30 g) baking powder

1½ teaspoons salt

1½ teaspoons ground cinnamon

1 teaspoon ground nutmeg

1 teaspoon grated orange zest

1 teaspoon ground ginger

WET INGREDIENTS:

4 cups (940 ml) milk

1 cup (225 g) (2 sticks) unsalted butter, melted

4 large eggs

1 teaspoon vanilla extract

—

Serves 4 to 6

In a large bowl, combine the milk, melted butter, eggs, and vanilla until well blended. Stir in the dry ingredients. Allow the batter to rest for 5 minutes before cooking in your waffle iron according to the manufacturer's instructions. Cool the cooked waffles on a rack.

TO PACKAGE AS A MIX: Place all of the dry ingredients in the freezer bag. Seal the bag and shake it gently to combine the ingredients. Store in the freezer.

FREEZING: Place the cooked waffles in the freezer bag and store in the freezer.

TO SERVE: Reheat frozen waffles (no need to thaw) in the toaster or toaster oven.

Bulk-Batch Pancakes

One thing I love about pancakes is that I can vary the batter recipe as well as the toppings to suit my mood or whatever's in the pantry. I've even been known to prepare them for a quick dinner when my other plans don't pan out. You can combine the dry ingredients in this bulk pancake recipe ahead of time for a mix that can be stored in the pantry or freezer. Or you can cook and cool the pancakes, wrap them in stacks of three, and store them in the freezer. Simply reheat cooked pancakes in the microwave or oven before serving. If you decide to package the recipe as a mix, be sure to mark the bag with a list of the wet ingredients to add right before cooking, as well as the cooking instructions.

Packaging: Quart-size (1 L) zip-top freezer bag or plastic wrap and gallon-size (4 L) zip-top freezer bags

DRY INGREDIENTS:

1½ cups (180 g) unbleached all-purpose flour

1½ cups (180 g) whole-wheat pastry flour

¼ cup (50 g) sugar

1 tablespoon baking powder

1 teaspoon baking soda

1 teaspoon salt

WET INGREDIENTS:

3 to 3½ cups (705 to 825 ml) buttermilk

2 large eggs

⅓ cup (75 g) unsalted butter, melted

Melted butter, for the griddle

—

Serves 4 to 6

In a large bowl, combine the buttermilk, eggs, and melted butter, blending well. Stir in the dry ingredients. There may be a few small lumps, but that's fine. Add some more buttermilk if the batter is too thick.

Heat a large skillet or griddle over medium heat until a few droplets of water sizzle when sprinkled onto the cooking surface. Brush the griddle with melted butter. Pour the batter onto the griddle in ¼-cup (60 ml) portions.

Cook the pancakes until bubbles form in the batter and start to pop. Flip the pancakes with a pancake turner. Brush the cooked tops of the cakes with more melted butter. Cook a minute or two more. Stack on a plate and continue until all are cooked.

TO PACKAGE AS A MIX: Place all of the dry ingredients in the quart-size (1 L) freezer bag. Seal the bag and shake it gently to combine. Store in the freezer.

FREEZING: Cool completely. Wrap pancakes in plastic wrap in stacks of three and place in the large freezer bag. Freeze.

TO THAW AND SERVE: Thaw the pancakes in the refrigerator or on the counter. Reheat in the microwave or oven until hot.

Oatmeal–Chocolate Chip Pancakes

These delicious, whole-grain pancakes are reminiscent of oatmeal–chocolate chip cookies, with a tad less guilt. See the previous recipe for recommendations on how to store both a pancake mix and cooked pancakes.

Packaging: Quart-size (1 L) zip-top freezer bag or plastic wrap and gallon-size (4 L) zip-top freezer bags

DRY INGREDIENTS:

1 cup (120 g) unbleached all-purpose flour

1 cup (120 g) whole-wheat pastry flour

1 cup (120 g) oat flour

½ cup (40 g) quick-cooking oats

¼ cup (56 g) brown sugar

1 tablespoon baking powder

1 teaspoon baking soda

1 teaspoon salt

½ cup (88 g) mini chocolate chips

WET INGREDIENTS:

3½ cups (825 ml) buttermilk

2 large eggs

⅓ cup (80 ml) vegetable oil

1 teaspoon vanilla extract

1 teaspoon grated orange zest

Butter, for the griddle

—
Serves 4 to 6

In a large bowl, combine the buttermilk, eggs, oil, vanilla, and orange zest, blending well. Add the dry ingredients, whisking until smooth. There may be a few lumps, but that's fine. Add some more buttermilk if the batter is too thick, or add 1 to 2 tablespoons (8 or 16 g) of flour if it is too thin.

Heat a large skillet or griddle over medium heat until a few droplets of water sizzle when sprinkled onto the cooking surface. Brush the griddle with melted butter. Pour the batter onto the griddle in ¼-cup (60 ml) portions.

Cook the pancakes until bubbles form in the batter and start to pop. Flip the pancakes with a pancake turner. Brush the cooked tops of the pancakes with more melted butter. Cook a minute or two more. Stack on a plate and continue until all are cooked.

TO PACKAGE AS A MIX: Place all of the dry ingredients in the quart-size (1 L) freezer bag. Seal the bag and shake it gently to combine the ingredients. Store in the freezer.

FREEZING: Cool completely. Wrap pancakes in plastic wrap in stacks of three and place in the large freezer bag. Freeze.

TO THAW AND SERVE: Thaw the pancakes in the refrigerator or on the counter. Reheat in the microwave or oven until hot.

Cinnamon French Toast Dippers

French toast is a tasty way to make use of day-old bread. With this recipe you can prepare a large batch of this crispy, crunchy, battered bread at one time, making it a perfect recipe for a crowd. I've updated a vintage recipe by stirring in some spices and using large French rolls sliced on the diagonal, which creates ideal "dippers."

Packaging: Gallon-size (4 L) zip-top freezer bag

5 large eggs

1 cup (235 ml) milk

1½ tablespoons (18 g) brown sugar

½ teaspoon salt

1 teaspoon vanilla extract

¼ teaspoon grated orange zest

½ teaspoon ground cinnamon

Three 8-inch (20.3 cm) French or sub rolls, sliced on the diagonal into 8 slices each

—

Serves 6 to 8

Preheat the oven to 500°F (250°C or gas mark 10). Line 2 to 3 baking sheets with parchment paper or silicone baking mats.

In a wide, shallow dish, mix the eggs, milk, brown sugar, salt, vanilla, orange zest, and cinnamon until well blended.

Dip both sides of the bread pieces into the egg mixture and arrange them on the prepared baking sheets.

Bake the bread slices until the undersides are golden, about 5 minutes. Turn the slices over. Bake until the bread is golden brown, or for 2 to 5 more minutes. Watch carefully to prevent burning.

FREEZING: Cool the French toast dippers completely on a wire rack. Place the dippers in the zip-top freezer bag and freeze.

TO SERVE: Preheat the oven to 375°F (190°C or gas mark 5). Place the frozen dippers (no need to thaw) on an ungreased baking sheet. Bake until heated through, for about 8 to 10 minutes. You can warm smaller quantities in the toaster or toaster oven.

Maple-Oat Waffles

These tasty waffles get even better under cold storage. The tang of the buttermilk mellows and the maple flavor shines through. Full of whole grains, they are a hearty way to start your morning. Serve them with butter and a little more maple syrup to make the day sing. Prepare the dry ingredients as a mix, or cook and freeze the waffles to reheat later for breakfasts on the go. If you decide to package the recipe as a mix, be sure to mark the bag with a list of the wet ingredients to add right before cooking, as well as the cooking instructions.

Packaging: Gallon-size (4 L) zip-top freezer bag

DRY INGREDIENTS:

2½ cups (300 g) unbleached all-purpose flour

2 cups (240 g) whole-wheat pastry flour

1 cup (120 g) oat flour

½ cup (40 g) quick-cooking oats

¼ cup (60 g) baking powder

1½ teaspoons salt

WET INGREDIENTS:

5 cups (1175 ml) buttermilk

1 cup (225 g) (2 sticks) unsalted butter, melted

¼ cup (60 ml) maple syrup

4 large eggs

—

Serves 4 to 6

In a large bowl, combine the dry ingredients with the wet ingredients. Allow the batter to rest for 5 minutes before cooking in your waffle iron according to the manufacturer's instructions. Cool the cooked waffles on a rack.

TO PACKAGE AS A MIX: Place all of the dry ingredients in the freezer bag. Seal the bag and shake it gently to combine the ingredients. Store in the freezer.

FREEZING: Place the cooked waffles in the labeled freezer bag and store in the freezer.

TO SERVE: Reheat frozen waffles (no need to thaw) in the toaster or toaster oven.

Lemon-and-Honey Flax Waffles

Talk about your day-brighteners! These waffles positively buzz with honey and lemon zest. The touch of flax brings fiber, antioxidants, and omega-3s to the table. These waffles are out of this world when served with berries and freshly whipped cream. Prepare the dry ingredients as a mix, or cook and freeze the waffles to reheat later for breakfasts on the go. If you decide to package the recipe as a mix, be sure to mark the bag with a list of the wet ingredients to add right before cooking, as well as the cooking instructions.

Packaging: Gallon-size (4 L) zip-top freezer bag

DRY INGREDIENTS:

3 cups (360 g) whole-wheat pastry flour

3 cups (360 g) unbleached all-purpose flour

¼ cup (30 g) baking powder

½ tablespoon salt

WET INGREDIENTS:

3½ cups (825 ml) milk

1 cup (235 ml) olive oil

3 large eggs

¼ cup (80 g) honey

1 tablespoon ground flax seed meal, combined with 3 tablespoons (45 ml) water

Grated zest of 1 lemon

—
Serves 4 to 6

In a large bowl, combine the dry ingredients with the wet ingredients. Allow the batter to rest for 5 minutes before cooking in your waffle iron according to the manufacturer's instructions. Cool the cooked waffles on a rack.

TO PACKAGE AS A MIX: Place all of the dry ingredients in the freezer bag. Seal the bag and shake it gently to combine the ingredients. Store in the freezer.

FREEZING: Place the cooked waffles in the freezer bag and store in the freezer.

TO SERVE: Reheat frozen waffles (no need to thaw) in the toaster or toaster oven.

Bacon-Cheddar Egg Bake for a Crowd

The egg bake is a fantastic make-ahead breakfast dish. It's basically bread, cheese, and cooked meat and/or vegetables soaked in a custard mixture, refrigerated overnight, and then baked in the morning. An egg bake is ideal to serve for brunch or, paired with a salad, as an elegant lunch. Egg dishes also freeze well, further freeing up your time. You can customize the egg bakes by adding different cheeses, meats, or precooked vegetables.

Packaging: One 9 × 13-inch (23 × 33 cm) baking dish with lid

6 cups (300 g) soft bread cubes

1⅓ cups (160 g) shredded cheddar cheese

4 slices bacon, cooked and chopped

9 large eggs, beaten

2 cups (470 ml) milk

¼ teaspoon freshly ground black pepper

—
Serves 6 to 8

Grease the baking dish. Spread the bread cubes across the bottom of the dish. Sprinkle the cheese and bacon over the bread cubes.

In a large bowl, combine the eggs, milk, and black pepper. Pour the egg mixture over the bread and cheese.

FREEZING: Cover and freeze.

TO THAW AND SERVE: Thaw the casserole in the refrigerator. Preheat the oven to 350°F (180°C or gas mark 4). Bake for 45 minutes to 1 hour, or until the top is puffy and a tester inserted in the center comes out clean.

Eggs Florentine Casserole

Breakfast has always been an enjoyable meal for our family. One of my favorite morning meals is this easy make-ahead casserole. It was served to my husband and me at a little bed and breakfast where we stayed on our honeymoon. It's a delicious way to get your children to eat spinach. Thanks to hearty portions of rich cheeses, it is both filling and flavorful.

Packaging: One 9 × 13-inch (23 × 33 cm) baking dish with lid or two 8-inch (20.3 cm) round baking dishes with lids

9 large eggs

16 ounces (454 g) cottage cheese

2 cups (240 g) shredded Swiss cheese

2 cups (240 g) crumbled feta cheese

One 10-ounce (280 g) package frozen chopped spinach, thawed and squeezed dry

—
Serves 6 to 10

Spray the baking dish(es) with nonstick cooking spray.

In a large bowl, beat the eggs. Add the cheeses and stir to combine well. Stir in the spinach. Pour the mixture into the prepared dish(es).

FREEZING: Cover and freeze.

TO THAW AND SERVE: Thaw the casserole in the refrigerator. Preheat the oven to 350°F (180°C or gas mark 4). Bake the casserole for 45 minutes to 1 hour, or until the eggs are cooked through. Cool slightly before cutting into squares. Serve hot or warm.

Buttered French Toast Casserole with Almonds and Ginger

A breakfast casserole is one of the easiest ways to start the morning. This elegant dish is bursting with color and sweetness from the cranberries and raisins, crunch from the almonds, and a little kick from the ginger. Leftovers are delicious served cold. For a crisper texture, omit the dried fruit and leave the dish uncovered for the entire baking time. Use a softer, Italian-style bread rather than a crusty French loaf for this dish, and serve with maple syrup, if you like.

Packaging: One 9 × 13-inch (23 × 33 cm) baking dish with lid

1 loaf Italian or brioche bread, 14 to 16 inches long (35.6 to 40.6 cm), sliced into 1½-inch (3.8 cm) slices

¼ cup (56 g) (½ stick) unsalted butter, softened

¼ cup (38 g) golden raisins or dark raisins, or a combination

2 tablespoons (16 g) dried cranberries

2 tablespoons (18 g) sliced almonds

2 tablespoons chopped crystallized ginger

3 large eggs, beaten

1 cup (235 ml) half-and-half

¼ cup (50 g) sugar

2 tablespoons (16 g) unbleached all-purpose flour

—

Serves 4 to 6

Spray the baking dish with nonstick cooking spray.

Butter the bread slices on one side and fit the slices, buttered side up, in the bottom of the prepared baking dish.

Sprinkle the raisins, cranberries, almonds, and ginger over the top of the bread.

In a bowl, combine the eggs, half-and-half, sugar, and flour, whisking well to combine. Pour the egg mixture over the bread slices.

FREEZING: Cover and freeze.

TO THAW AND SERVE: Thaw the casserole in the refrigerator. Preheat the oven to 350°F (180°C or gas mark 4). Bake, covered, for 25 minutes, then remove the cover and bake for 20 more minutes.

Savory Ham and Swiss Clafouti

A clafouti is traditionally a fruit-and-custard dessert. However, savory clafouti has recently arrived on the scene. Similar to a crustless quiche, this rich ham-and-cheese custard makes an elegant breakfast or brunch entrée.

Packaging: One 9-inch (23 cm) baking dish with lid, heavy-duty aluminum foil

3 large eggs

1½ cups (355 ml) cream or half-and-half

1 teaspoon Dijon mustard

1 tablespoon chopped fresh parsley or 1 teaspoon dried parsley flakes

⅛ teaspoon freshly ground black pepper

1 cup (120 g) shredded Swiss cheese mixed with 2 tablespoons (16 g) unbleached all-purpose flour

1¾ cups diced ham (about 8 ounces [224 g])

—

Serves 4 to 6

Grease the baking dish.

In a large bowl, beat the eggs. Stir in the cream, Dijon mustard, parsley, and pepper. Stir in the shredded cheese and diced ham. Pour the egg mixture into the prepared baking dish.

FREEZING: Place the baking dish flat in the freezer. Freeze until firm. Cover the frozen clafouti or wrap well with foil. Return to the freezer.

TO THAW AND SERVE: Thaw the clafouti in the refrigerator. Preheat the oven to 350°F (180°C or gas mark 4). Bake the thawed clafouti, uncovered, for 30 to 45 minutes. Alternatively, bake the frozen clafouti for 45 minutes to 1 hour, or until a knife inserted in the center comes out clean.

Chile and Sausage Oven Frittata

This oven-baked egg dish is full of flavor from the sausage and green chiles. It is also a breeze to prepare. Mix up and freeze several at a time, and enjoy this easy, protein-packed main dish later. The frittata also makes a delicious and simple lunch or dinner when served with a side salad or a bowl of soup.

Packaging: One 9-inch (23 cm) deep-dish pie plate, heavy-duty aluminum foil

4 ounces (112 g) sweet Italian sausage, casings removed

¾ cup (90 g) shredded Monterey Jack cheese mixed with 1 tablespoon unbleached all-purpose flour

One 4-ounce (112 g) can diced green chiles

6 large eggs, beaten

½ teaspoon ground cumin

⅛ teaspoon freshly ground black pepper

1 tablespoon chopped fresh cilantro

—

Serves 4 to 6

In a large skillet over medium-high heat, cook the sausage until no longer pink, breaking up the chunks with the back of a spoon. Drain the sausage and let cool.

Grease the deep-dish pie plate. Sprinkle the sausage, cheese, and chiles over the bottom of the pie plate.

In a large bowl, beat the eggs. Stir in the cumin and pepper. Pour the egg mixture into the pie plate. Sprinkle the cilantro over the top.

FREEZING: Place the pie plate flat in the freezer. Freeze until firm. Cover the frozen frittata with foil. Return to the freezer.

TO THAW AND SERVE: Thaw frittata in the refrigerator. Preheat the oven to 400°F (200°C or gas mark 6). Remove the foil from the frittata and bake it for 20 to 30 minutes, or until the eggs are set.

Breakfast Smoothies

While blending a smoothie doesn't take that long, it's nice to be able to grab a quick, cold snack or breakfast. Freezer smoothies are just the ticket! Dishwasher- and microwave-safe 8-ounce (224 g) plastic freezer jars with screw-on lids are perfect for storing freezer smoothies.

Making smoothies can be really simple. Just blend different combinations of fruits, juices, and ice. To make dairy-based smoothies, add yogurt and/or milk. Or use soy milk or almond milk, for creaminess without dairy. I even use homemade fruit jam to flavor milk-based smoothies. Test out some of your favorite fruits and see what combinations you like best. And then keep your freezer stocked for all sorts of cool snacking.

A smoothie is great to pack in the lunch box or to grab and go. Thaw in the refrigerator for 4 hours before serving or on the counter for about an hour, or microwave it for 20 seconds on 50 percent power for a perfect slushy consistency.

SMOOTHIE BOWL VARIATION: Smoothie bowls have seen quite a bit of popularity in recent years. Consider packing your smoothie as a bowl, not a drink. Blend the smoothie on the thicker side and pour into plastic containers. Top with your favorite frozen fruit, nuts, and seeds. Cover and freeze.

The Red Banana

There's a smoothie bar in Santa Barbara that serves up some of the best smoothies on the planet, including the Red Banana, a milk-based smoothie with strawberries and bananas. It is delicious simplicity.

Packaging: Six plastic freezer jars with lids

2½ cups (590 ml) nonfat milk

1 cup (170 g) sliced strawberries

2 bananas, broken into pieces

—

Serves 6

Mix the milk, strawberries, and bananas in the blender until smooth. Pour the mixture into the freezer jars, leaving ½ inch (1.3 cm) headspace.

FREEZING: Cover the jars and freeze.

TO THAW AND SERVE: Thaw smoothies in the refrigerator for 4 hours or on the counter for about an hour, or microwave them for 20 seconds on 50 percent power. Serve immediately.

The Red Orange

This nondairy fruit-based smoothie is a great way to get one of your five daily servings of produce. The riper the strawberries, the sweeter the treat. Add a teaspoon or two of honey to adjust the sweetness, if desired.

Packaging: Six plastic freezer jars with lids

2 cups (470 ml) orange juice

2 cups (340 g) sliced strawberries

½ cup (120 ml) raspberry-grape juice blend

1 to 2 teaspoons honey (optional)

—
Serves 6

Mix the orange juice, strawberries, and raspberry-grape juice in the blender until smooth. Taste and adjust the sweetness if necessary by adding honey. Pour the mixture into the freezer jars, leaving ½ inch (1.3 cm) headspace.

FREEZING: Cover the jars and freeze.

TO THAW AND SERVE: Thaw smoothies in the refrigerator for 4 hours or on the counter for about an hour, or microwave them for 20 seconds on 50 percent power. Serve immediately.

The Blue Maple

This milky treat features blueberries and gets a little zip from the maple syrup.

Packaging: Six plastic freezer jars with lids

2 cups (470 ml) milk

1½ cups (225 g) blueberries

¾ cup (180 g) plain yogurt

2 tablespoons (30 ml) maple syrup

—
Serves 6

Mix the milk, blueberries, yogurt, and maple syrup in the blender until smooth. Pour the mixture into the freezer jars, leaving ½ inch (1.3 cm) headspace.

FREEZING: Cover the jars and freeze.

TO THAW AND SERVE: Thaw smoothies in the refrigerator for 4 hours or on the counter for about and hour, or microwave them for 20 seconds on 50 percent power. Serve immediately.

The Blue Pineapple

Canned pineapple and fresh blueberries blend beautifully with plain yogurt for a nutritious smoothie.

Packaging: Six plastic freezer jars with lids

One 20-ounce (560 g) can sliced or chunk pineapple in juice

1 cup (150 g) blueberries

8 ounces (224 g) plain yogurt

—
Serves 6

Mix the pineapple, blueberries, and yogurt in the blender until smooth. Pour the mixture into the freezer jars, leaving ½ inch (1.3 cm) headspace.

FREEZING: Cover the jars and freeze.

TO THAW AND SERVE: Thaw smoothies in the refrigerator for 4 hours or on the counter for about an hour, or microwave them for 20 seconds on 50 percent power. Serve immediately.

Milk and Honey Granola

Granola can be a pretty pricey grocery store item. However, it is very easy to make this breakfast cereal yourself at home. If you can buy the ingredients in bulk and/or on sale, you will enjoy further savings. An added benefit is that you can add whatever nuts and seeds you like. This basic recipe is flavored with honey and cooks slowly in the oven. Enjoy it as a breakfast cereal, in parfaits layered with yogurt and fruit, or just for snacking.

Packaging: Plastic containers with lids or gallon-size (4 L) zip-top freezer bag

5 cups (400 g) old-fashioned rolled oats (do not use quick-cooking oats)

½ cup (60 g) wheat bran

1 cup (80 g) wheat germ

½ cup (72 g) sesame seeds

½ teaspoon salt

1 cup (320 g) honey

½ cup (120 ml) vegetable oil

½ cup (60 g) powdered nonfat milk

2 teaspoons lemon zest

—
Serves 6 to 8

Preheat the oven to 300°F (150°C or gas mark 2). Grease a large, rimmed baking sheet or line it with parchment paper.

In a very large bowl, combine the oats, wheat bran, wheat germ, sesame seeds, and salt. In a separate bowl, combine the honey, oil, powdered milk, and lemon zest. Pour the wet mixture over the dry and toss to coat evenly.

Spread the mixture on the prepared baking sheet. Bake for 40 to 45 minutes, stirring every 15 minutes. Do not let the mixture brown too much.

Remove the pan from the oven and allow the granola to cool completely.

FREEZING: Store in a plastic container or freezer bag in the freezer.

TO THAW AND SERVE: Thaw the granola in its container on the counter.

Raspberry Baked Oatmeal

I was a skeptic about baked oatmeal, but Lynn's Kitchen Adventures made me a believer. My friend Lynn has created over TWENTY different versions of baked oatmeal! This raspberry-studded version is one I adapted from her standard, based on what I had on hand and what my kids liked. I was so pleased to see how freezer-friendly these oatmeal casseroles are!

Packaging: One 9 × 13-inch (23 × 33 cm) baking pan with lid

3 cups (240 g) old-fashioned oats

¼ cup (60 g) brown sugar

2 teaspoons baking powder

¾ teaspoon salt

½ cup (112 g) applesauce

½ cup (112 g) plain yogurt

½ cup (120 ml) nonfat milk

¼ cup (60 ml) oil or (56 g) butter

1 teaspoon vanilla extract

2 eggs

2 cups (300 g) raspberries
(can use frozen, no need to thaw)

**WHEN READY TO SERVE,
YOU WILL NEED:**

Heavy cream, whipped or plain

—

Serves 8 to 10

Grease a 9 × 13-inch (23 × 33 cm) baking pan.

In a large mixing bowl, combine the oats, brown sugar, baking powder, and salt.

In a second mixing bowl, whisk together the applesauce, yogurt, milk, oil, vanilla, eggs.

Pour the wet ingredients onto the dry, and add the raspberries. Fold gently to combine. Spoon the mixture into the prepared pan.

FREEZING: Cover and freeze.

TO THAW AND SERVE: Thaw the casserole overnight in the refrigerator. Preheat the oven to 350°F (180°C or gas mark 4) and bake for 30 to 40 minutes, or until golden. To bake from frozen, add 10 to 15 minutes to the baking time.

CHAPTER 6
Breads and Baked Goods

Basic Pizza Dough

Many grocery stores now sell pizza dough in the refrigerated section. But it's not difficult to make your own. By doing so, you can customize the ingredients and save money. To speed things up, I use a bread machine or stand mixer to prepare the dough. This gives me a more consistent texture and keeps the kitchen cleaner. But you can very easily mix and knead this dough by hand, if you prefer.

Preparing the dough takes about 2 hours from start to finish. However, I can break up that prep time by mixing and freezing the dough one day and letting it thaw and rise another day. This helps me use my time in the kitchen more efficiently.

For bulk dough making, I usually start one batch in the bread machine and then get my KitchenAid stand mixer going on another. I freeze the dough after it has risen for only 30 minutes, placing each greased dough ball in a plastic sandwich bag and then storing them in a larger freezer bag or paired with other ingredients in a pizza kit.

Packaging: Zip-top sandwich bags, gallon-size (4 L) zip-top freezer bag

1½ cups (355 ml) water

¼ cup (60 ml) olive oil

2 tablespoons (40 g) honey or (25 g) sugar

4½ cups (540 g) unbleached all-purpose flour (you can substitute up to 1 cup [120 g] whole-wheat flour for an equivalent amount of all-purpose flour)

1 tablespoon (18 g) salt

1 tablespoon active dry yeast

—
Makes enough dough for four 12-inch (30.5 cm) pizzas or 8 individual-size pizzas

IF MAKING DOUGH IN A BREAD MACHINE: Combine all of the ingredients in the bread machine pan in the order recommended by the manufacturer. Set the machine to the dough cycle and start it, checking after 10 minutes to make sure all of the ingredients have been incorporated and are not stuck to the side of the pan. Once the mixing cycle is complete, allow the dough to rise for 30 minutes.

IF MAKING DOUGH IN A STAND MIXER: Combine the water and honey in the bowl of the stand mixer. Sprinkle the yeast over the top and allow it to proof for 5 minutes. Add the oil, 2 cups (240 g) of the flour, and the salt. Fit the mixer with the dough hook and beat on low speed. Once the dough starts to come together, 1 to 2 minutes, increase the speed a notch. Knead the dough, gradually adding more flour until a dough ball forms. Knead the dough 2 minutes more. Transfer the dough to a greased bowl and turn it to coat it with oil. Allow the dough to rise for 30 minutes.

IF MAKING DOUGH BY HAND: In a large bowl, combine the water, oil, honey, and yeast, and allow to proof for 5 minutes. Add the flour and salt, stirring with a wooden spoon until a stiff dough forms. Turn the dough out onto a lightly floured surface and knead for 5 minutes, or until the dough has a smooth, elastic feel. Add more flour if necessary. Transfer the dough to a greased bowl and turn it to coat it with oil. Allow the dough to rise for 30 minutes.

(continued)

TO FINISH THE DOUGH: When the dough is ready, use greased hands to divide it into 4 or 8 portions, as desired. Shape each portion into a ball. Place each dough ball into a sandwich bag and freeze immediately. The dough will continue to rise and you want to arrest that process, so the sooner it is frozen, the better.

FREEZING: Package the dough balls with other pizza ingredients to make kits or in one large zip-top freezer bag.

TO THAW AND SERVE: Remove the frozen dough from the freezer. Remove the dough from the bag and place in a greased bowl; if thawing more than one dough ball, place on a greased baking pan. Allow the dough to rise for 6 to 8 hours in the refrigerator or for 3 hours at room temperature. If the dough has risen in the refrigerator, let it sit at room temperature for 30 minutes before forming, topping, and baking.

Tomato and Herb Pizza Sauce

This flavorful sauce comes together in minutes. Inspired by the sauce at California Pizza Kitchen, it is a delicious topping for pizzas and dip for Calzones (pages 122 and 123) and French Bread Pizza Dippers (page 124).

Packaging: Plastic containers with lids

¼ cup (60 ml) olive oil

2 teaspoons minced garlic

One 28-ounce (784 g) can petite diced tomatoes with juices

3 tablespoons chopped fresh basil or 1 tablespoon dried basil

1 teaspoon salt

½ teaspoon dried oregano

¼ teaspoon red pepper flakes

One 6-ounce (168 g) can tomato paste

—
Makes about 4½ cups (1060 ml)

In a large saucepan, heat the olive oil over medium heat until shimmering. Stir in the garlic and cook until just barely browned.

Add the tomatoes, basil, salt, oregano, and red pepper flakes. Simmer until the juices have started to evaporate slightly, about 10 minutes.

Stir in the tomato paste and cook 3 minutes more. This is a chunky sauce. Use it as is or puree it with an immersion blender or in a food processor. Let cool.

FREEZING: Divide the sauce into desired portions in plastic containers. Cool completely. Cover and chill in the refrigerator before freezing.

TO THAW AND SERVE: Thaw the sauce in the refrigerator. Use as a topping or dip.

Pizza Night Is a Highlight of Our Week—with Pizza Kits on Hand

For many folks, pizza night is a great way to kick off the weekend, celebrate a team's victory, or otherwise enjoy a casual meal with friends and family. And many of us rely on the pizza parlor or the frozen-food section of the grocery store to provide this culinary delight.

But homemade pizza can be as good as or better than commercial versions. And if you've got a few pizza kits in your freezer, you'll be set for a delicious dinner with a minimal amount of work.

I often spend Friday afternoons assembling the makings of homemade pizza, which I bake in the oven or cook on the grill. We enjoy it with vegetable dippers and homemade ranch dressing or a mixed salad. Then after kitchen cleanup (or not), we watch a movie and officially enter the weekend.

Most members of my younger crew prefer simple cheese or pepperoni pizzas, while the more mature ones in our family opt for the Jalapeño Burn Pizza (page 129).

The trick to making these pizza nights relaxing is to have pizza kits at the ready. Homemade sauce, pizza dough, shredded cheese, and other toppings can be prepared ahead and stored in the freezer, ready to grab and thaw in the refrigerator.

All kinds of frozen meal components can come together in a beautiful way for pizza night. A barbecue sauce pairs well with shredded chicken on one pizza, while a homemade sauce and shredded cheese come together on another. It's easy to make several kinds of pizza on one night if you have the fixings portioned and ready to go.

Creating pizza kits also helps you make good use of your bulk shopping items, like those large bags of cheese you might buy at a warehouse club. Don't fear the 5-pound (2270 g) bag of cheese. That's the most economical way to buy shredded mozzarella. Simply divide the cheese into quart-size (1 L) freezer bags when you bring it home. Put ½ pound (224 g, about 2 cups) of cheese in each bag, enough for a pizza, depending on how cheesy you like it. Stash the bags in the freezer or, for even greater efficiency, combine them with other components in a pizza kit.

The easiest way to put together pizza kits is to bundle all the components together in a gallon-size (4 L) zip-top freezer bag. Label the bag (be sure to note what kind of pizza fixings it contains), and include a bag of pizza dough, a bag of cheese, a container of sauce, and any other freezable toppings you would like.

Pepperoni Calzones

A calzone is simply a pizza folded in half. Make them with any number of fillings, provided that the fillings do not have a lot of water in them, which would make the crust soggy. Since these are baked prior to freezing, they make great snacks or lunches: Simply reheat them in a toaster oven or microwave.

Packaging: Plastic wrap, two gallon-size (4 L) zip-top freezer bags

1 batch Basic Pizza Dough (page 119), prepared through step 1

Cornmeal for sprinkling

4 cups (480 g) shredded mozzarella cheese

Two 6-ounce (168 g) packages sliced pepperoni (about 64 slices)

WHEN READY TO SERVE, YOU WILL NEED:

Easy Slow Cooker Red Sauce (page 89) or other favorite red sauce, warmed

—
Serves 8

Once the pizza dough is mixed, allow it to rise for 1 hour or until doubled in bulk.

Preheat the oven to 475°F (240°C or gas mark 9). Grease 2 or 3 baking sheets and sprinkle them with cornmeal.

Transfer the dough to a lightly floured surface and divide it into 8 equal portions. Form each portion into a tight ball. Once all the portions are formed, flatten each one into a 6- to 8-inch (15 to 20.3 cm) round.

Sprinkle ½ cup (60 g) mozzarella cheese over half of each dough round, leaving a ½-inch (1.3 cm) border around the edge. Arrange 8 slices of pepperoni over the cheese.

Fold the other half of the dough over the pepperoni and press to seal the edges. You should have a half-moon shape. Gently turn the bottom crust over the top in sections to further seal the rounded edge. As you work your way around the edge of the dough, each turned-up section should build on the previous one, creating a type of braided effect.

Place all the formed calzones on the prepared baking sheets. Cut 2 or 3 slits in the top of each one. Bake for 10 to 12 minutes or until crisp. Remove from the baking sheets and cool on a rack.

FREEZING: Wrap each cooled calzone in plastic wrap. Package 4 calzones in each freezer bag and store in the freezer.

TO THAW AND SERVE: Thaw calzones in the refrigerator overnight. Preheat the oven to 350°F (180°C or gas mark 4). Unwrap the calzones and reheat for 5 to 10 minutes, or until heated through. Serve with the warmed sauce for dipping.

Spinach and Cheese Calzones

Spinach and ricotta are natural partners and combine into a delicious filling in these calzones, which make an elegant appetizer or light main course. Pair them with Tomato Sauce with Oregano and Kalamata Olives (page 88) for a fresh twist. These are great to pack in lunches and reheat at work or school.

Packaging: Plastic wrap, two gallon-size (4 L) zip-top freezer bags

1 batch Basic Pizza Dough (page 119), prepared through step 1

Cornmeal for sprinkling

2 cups (450 g) ricotta cheese

One 16-ounce (454 g) package frozen chopped spinach, thawed and squeezed dry

1 tablespoon Jamie's Spice Mix (page 30)

WHEN READY TO SERVE, YOU WILL NEED:

Tomato Sauce with Oregano and Kalamata Olives (page 88) or other favorite tomato sauce, warmed

—
Serves 8

Once the pizza dough is mixed, allow it to rise for 1 hour or until doubled in bulk.

Preheat the oven to 475°F (240°C or gas mark 9). Grease 2 or 3 baking sheets and sprinkle them with cornmeal.

Transfer the dough to a lightly floured surface and divide it into 8 equal portions. Form each portion into a tight ball. Once all the portions are formed, flatten each one into a 6- to 8-inch (15 to 20.3 cm) round.

In a large bowl, combine the ricotta cheese, spinach, and spice mix. Divide the cheese mixture among the 8 dough rounds, spreading it over half of each dough round and leaving a ½-inch (1.3 cm) border around the edge.

Fold the other half of dough over the cheese filling and press to seal the edges. You should have a half-moon shape. Gently turn the bottom crust over the top in portions to further seal the rounded edge. As you work your way around the edge of the dough, each turned-up section should build on the previous one, creating a type of braided effect.

Place all the formed calzones on the prepared baking sheets. Cut 2 or 3 slits in the top of each one. Bake for 10 to 12 minutes or until crisp. Remove from the baking sheets and cool on a rack.

FREEZING: Wrap each calzone in plastic wrap. Package 4 calzones in each freezer bag and store in the freezer.

TO THAW AND SERVE: Thaw calzones in the refrigerator overnight. Preheat the oven to 350°F (180°C or gas mark 4). Unwrap the calzones and reheat for 5 to 10 minutes, or until heated through. Serve with the warmed sauce for dipping.

French Bread Pizza Dippers

I love to experiment with pizza, and one way to do that is with different pizza bases. Large flour tortillas work in a pinch for quick lunchtime thin-crust pizzas. And bagel and English muffin pizzas have long been a kids' standby. When I set out to find a way to make French bread pizza work for freezer meals, the answer was a baguette pizza "dipper." Similar in spirit to the tartine, or baguette spread with butter and jam that I dipped into my breakfast coffee when I lived in France, this is a pizza baguette spread with garlic butter and mozzarella cheese that's dipped in a homemade pizza sauce. The result is a deliciously crisp, cheesy pizza bread that waits happily in the freezer until a pizza craving hits.

Packaging: Gallon-size (4 L) zip-top freezer bag

¼ cup (56 g) (½ stick) salted butter, softened

1 teaspoon chopped garlic

1 traditional French baguette, about 24 inches (61 cm) long, cut into thirds and split horizontally

8 ounces (224 g) sliced mozzarella cheese

WHEN READY TO SERVE, YOU WILL NEED:

1 cup (235 ml) Tomato and Herb Pizza Sauce (page 120) or other favorite red sauce, warmed

—

Serves 2 generously

In a small mixing bowl, combine the butter and garlic. Spread the garlic butter on each of the six baguette pieces.

Layer the mozzarella cheese over the garlic butter.

FREEZING: Place the cheese-topped bread pieces in the freezer bag. Remove as much air as possible and seal. Freeze.

TO THAW AND SERVE: Thaw the bread in the refrigerator. Preheat the oven to 475°F (240°C or gas mark 9). Place the bread on a baking sheet. Bake for 5 to 10 minutes, until the cheese is melted and starting to brown slightly and the crust is crisp. Serve with the warmed sauce on the side for dipping.

Easy Make-Ahead Garlic Bread

While preparing homemade garlic bread is inarguably easy, it does take a few minutes. And sometimes you just want that garlic bread PRONTO. Win by keeping a few loaves stashed in the freezer, ready to throw on the grill or toss in the oven alongside the rest of the dinner. For a crispier top, unwrap the foil at the end of the baking time and broil the bread briefly.

Packaging: Heavy-duty aluminum foil

½ cup (112 g) (1 stick) unsalted butter, softened

2 cloves garlic, minced

1 tablespoon chopped fresh basil or oregano or 1 teaspoon dried basil or oregano (optional)

1½ teaspoons chopped fresh parsley or ½ teaspoon dried parsley flakes

1 large loaf French or Italian bread, halved lengthwise

—
Makes 1 large loaf

In a small bowl, combine the butter, garlic, basil (if using), and parsley.

Spread the butter in a thick layer over the surface of each bread half.

FREEZING: Put the two bread halves back together and wrap with foil. Freeze.

TO THAW AND SERVE: Thaw the bread in the refrigerator. Bake, still wrapped in foil, at 375°F (190°C or gas mark 5) for 15 to 25 minutes, depending on the density of the bread. Or bake the frozen bread for 35 to 40 minutes.

Lemon-Blueberry Scones

Lemons and blueberries are a classic flavor combination, and for good reason. They just burst with sunshiny flavor. What better way to start a morning than with fresh-baked lemony scones, popping with blueberries? Mix up a batch to freeze. On a busy morning, you can pull them from the freezer and pop them in the oven. They'll be ready in no time.

Packaging: Zip-top freezer bags (gallon size [4 L] for preformed or baked scones, quart size [1 L] for mix)

DRY INGREDIENTS:

3 cups (360 g) whole-wheat pastry flour

2 cups (240 g) unbleached all-purpose flour

1 cup (200 g) sugar

1 tablespoon baking powder

1 teaspoon baking soda

½ teaspoon salt

WET INGREDIENTS:

Grated zest of 1 lemon

1 cup (225 g) (2 sticks) unsalted butter, cut into cubes

2 cups (470 ml) buttermilk

1½ cups (225 g) frozen blueberries (no need to thaw)

—
Makes 12 scones

Line baking sheets with parchment paper.

In a large bowl, combine the dry ingredients and lemon zest. Cut in the butter with a pastry blender or two knives until coarse crumbs form. (To speed up the process, you can do this in batches in a food processor, then remove the mixture to a large bowl.)

Add the buttermilk and blueberries. Fold gently until combined. The dough will be sticky.

Turn the dough out onto a floured surface and fold 2 or 3 turns, or until the dough comes together.

Gently pat or roll the dough into a 1-inch (2.5 cm)-thick rectangle, taking care not to squash the berries. Cut the dough into 12 rectangles. Scones can be baked at this point.

TO PACKAGE AS A MIX: Place all of the dry ingredients in the quart-size (1 L) freezer bag. Seal the bag and shake it gently to combine the ingredients. Store in the pantry or freezer.

FREEZING: Place the unbaked scones on parchment-lined baking sheets and freeze until firm. Once the scones are firm, transfer them to the gallon-size (4 L) freezer bags, removing as much air as possible. Freeze. Baked scones can also be frozen in an airtight container or freezer bag.

TO SERVE: Preheat the oven to 375°F (190°C or gas mark 5). Bake scones for 20 minutes, or 25 minutes for frozen scones (no need to thaw). Cool and serve. Thaw prebaked scones in bags at room temperature.

Easy-Peasy Cheesy Pizza

This cheese pizza is delicious—and easy. It's utterly simple, but it still packs a punch of flavor. The combination of cheeses makes it especially delicious. My baby girl, now nine, deems it her favorite pizza EVER, though she does like to bake an egg on top from time to time.

Packaging: Quart- (1 L) or pint-size (470 ml) bag, snack-size bag, plastic container with lid or additional snack-size bag, gallon-size (4 L) zip-top freezer bag

¾ cup (90 g) shredded mozzarella cheese

¾ cup (90 g) shredded Monterey Jack cheese

¼ cup (25 g) Parmesan Herb Blend (page 130)

½ cup (120 ml) Tomato and Herb Pizza Sauce (page 120)

¼ batch frozen, bagged Basic Pizza Dough (page 119)

—

Makes one 12-inch (30.5 cm) pizza

Place the mozzarella and Jack cheeses in the quart- (1 L) or pint-size (470 ml) bag. Place the Parmesan Herb Blend in the snack-size bag. Place the pizza sauce in a plastic container or a snack-size bag.

Place the two bags of cheese and the container of sauce, along with the frozen pizza dough, in the gallon-size (4 L) zip-top freezer bag. Store in the freezer.

TO THAW AND SERVE: Remove the pizza kit from the freezer. Grease a medium bowl. Unwrap the pizza dough and place it in the greased bowl. Thaw it in the refrigerator for 6 to 8 hours, covered. Thaw the other items in the kit in the refrigerator. Preheat the oven to 475°F (240°C or gas mark 9). Allow the dough to sit at room temperature for about 30 minutes. Stretch the dough to fit a 12-inch (30.5 cm) pizza pan. Spread the sauce over the prepared dough. Sprinkle the mozzarella mixture over the sauce. Sprinkle the Parmesan Herb Blend over the top. Bake the pizza for 10 to 12 minutes, or until the crust is crisp and the cheese is melted and starting to brown. Cool slightly before slicing and serving.

Jalapeño Burn Pizza

Those who love spicy food will get a real kick out of this pizza. Red pepper flakes and sliced jalapeños offer heat, while the tomatoes refresh your palate and the cheese helps cool the burn. It's particularly good served with chopped fresh avocado added after the pizza comes out of the oven.

Packaging: Quart- (1 L) or pint-size (470 ml) bag, two snack-size bags, sandwich bag, gallon-size (4 L) zip-top freezer bag

1 cup (120 g) shredded mozzarella cheese

½ cup (60 g) shredded cheddar cheese

½ cup (80 g) chopped onion

2 jalapeño peppers, thinly sliced

1 cup (140 g) chopped cooked chicken

¼ batch frozen, bagged Basic Pizza Dough (page 119)

WHEN READY TO SERVE, YOU WILL NEED:

1 tablespoon (15 ml) olive oil

Red pepper flakes

1 medium tomato, diced

¼ cup (25 g) sliced black olives

1 medium avocado, peeled, pitted, and chopped

—

Makes one 12-inch (30.5 cm) pizza, serves 4

Place the mozzarella and cheddar cheeses in the quart- (1 L) or pint-size (470 ml) bag. Place the chopped onion in a snack-size bag. Place the sliced jalapeño in another snack-size bag. Place the chopped chicken in the sandwich bag and seal.

Place the bagged cheese, onion, jalapeño, and chicken, along with the bag of frozen pizza dough, in the gallon-size (4 L) zip-top freezer bag. Store in the freezer.

TO THAW AND SERVE: Remove the pizza kit from the freezer. Grease a medium bowl. Unwrap the pizza dough and place it in the greased bowl. Thaw it in the refrigerator for 6 to 8 hours, covered. Thaw the other items in the kit in the refrigerator. Preheat the oven to 475°F (240°C or gas mark 9). Allow the dough to sit at room temperature for about 30 minutes. Stretch the dough to fit a 12-inch (30.5 cm) pizza pan. Spread the oil over the prepared pizza dough. Sprinkle with red pepper flakes to taste and 1 cup (120 g) of the mozzarella mixture. Layer the chicken, tomato, onion, jalapeños, and black olives over the cheese. Sprinkle the remaining ½ cup (60 g) cheese over the top. Bake for 10 to 12 minutes, or until the crust is crisp and the cheese is melted and golden in spots. Cool slightly, sprinkle chopped avocado over the pizza, slice, and serve.

Parmesan Herb Blend

This mixture is delicious stirred into sauces, sprinkled on salads or steamed vegetables, or used to season herb butters. Toss hot cooked pasta with olive oil and a few tablespoons of this mixture for an easy side dish. Mix up a batch at the beginning of a freezer cooking session and use it to add instant flavor to a number of dishes, including Easy-Peasy Cheesy Pizza (page 128).

Packaging: Pint-size (470 ml) zip-top freezer bag or plastic container with lid

1 cup (100 g) grated Parmesan cheese

1 tablespoon chopped fresh parsley or 1 teaspoon dried parsley flakes

1 teaspoon garlic powder

¾ teaspoon chopped fresh basil or ¼ teaspoon dried basil

¼ teaspoon dried oregano

¼ teaspoon dried thyme

⅛ teaspoon freshly ground black pepper

—
Makes about 1 cup (100 g)

In a small bowl, gently mix all of the ingredients.

FREEZING: Freeze the cheese blend in a freezer bag or airtight container.

Cinnamon Banana Bread

I love baking banana bread in big batches. When you're rich in golden loaves fragrant with cinnamon and banana, it's easy to share—and to stash a few away for a rainy day. Baking in muffin tins can save you time and provide you with individual breads, ready to pack for work, school, or play.

Packaging: Plastic wrap, gallon-size (4 L) zip-top freezer bags

6 bananas, mashed

1½ cups (355 ml) half-and-half

3 large eggs

¾ cup (180 ml) vegetable oil or melted unsalted butter

2 cups (450 g) light or dark brown sugar

3 cups (360 g) unbleached all-purpose flour

3 cups (360 g) whole-wheat pastry flour

1 tablespoon baking powder

1½ teaspoons baking soda

1½ teaspoons salt

1½ teaspoons ground cinnamon

—
Makes four 9 × 5-inch (23 × 12.7 cm) loaves or 36 to 40 mini breads

Preheat the oven to 350°F (180°C or gas mark 4). Spray 4 loaf pans with nonstick cooking spray or line muffin tins with paper liners. You can bake some of both sizes, if you prefer.

In a very large bowl, blend the bananas, half-and-half, eggs, and oil until smooth. Add the brown sugar and stir, smoothing out any lumps.

Add the flours, baking powder, baking soda, salt, and cinnamon. Fold the wet and dry ingredients together just until mixed.

Pour the batter into the prepared pans. Bake the loaves for about 1 hour, or until a tester inserted in the center comes out clean. Bake the mini breads for 20 to 22 minutes, or until a tester inserted in the center comes out clean.

Transfer the pans to a rack and let cool for 10 minutes, then remove the breads from the pans and place on a rack to cool completely.

FREEZING: Wrap each cooled loaf in plastic wrap. Place two wrapped loaves in each freezer bag and freeze. Mini breads can be placed in freezer bags; remove as much air as possible before sealing the bags.

TO THAW AND SERVE: Thaw banana bread, wrapped, at room temperature for about 1 hour.

Raspberry Jam Cream Scones

My husband loves the raspberry scones at a certain coffee shop. I found a way to make them at home, and now I can freeze them and pop them in the oven at any time. Feel free to make scone "bites" by cutting the dough into smaller squares.

Packaging: Zip-top freezer bags (gallon size [4 L] for preformed or baked scones, quart size [1 L] for mix)

DRY INGREDIENTS:

2 cups (240 g) whole-wheat pastry flour

3 cups (360 g) unbleached all-purpose flour

1 cup (200 g) sugar

1 tablespoon baking powder

1 teaspoon baking soda

½ teaspoon salt

WET INGREDIENTS:

1 teaspoon grated orange zest

¾ cup (170 g) (1½ sticks) unsalted butter, cut into cubes

1¾ cups (415 ml) cream

⅓ cup (75 g) seedless raspberry jam

—
Makes 12 scones

Line baking sheets with parchment paper.

In a large bowl, combine dry ingredients and orange zest. Cut in the butter with a pastry blender or two knives until coarse crumbs form. (To speed up the process, do this in batches in a food processor, then transfer to a large bowl.)

Add the cream. Fold gently until combined. The dough will be sticky.

Turn the dough out onto a floured surface and fold 2 or 3 turns, or until the dough comes together.

Pat or roll the dough into a 1-inch (2.5 cm)-thick rectangle. Spread the jam over one half of the dough. Fold the side without jam over the jam side and press to flatten again to a 1-inch (2.5 cm) thickness. The jam and dough should swirl together a bit. Cut the dough into 12 rectangles. Scones can be baked at this point.

TO PACKAGE AS A MIX: Place all of the dry ingredients in the quart-size (1 L) freezer bag. Seal the bag and shake it gently to combine the ingredients. Store in the pantry or freezer.

FREEZING: Place the unbaked scones on parchment-lined baking sheets and freeze until firm. Once the scones are firm, transfer them to the gallon-size (4 L) freezer bags, removing as much air as possible. Freeze. Baked scones can also be frozen in an airtight container or freezer bag.

TO SERVE: Preheat the oven to 375°F (190°C or gas mark 5). Bake scones for 20 minutes, or 25 minutes for frozen scones (no need to thaw). Cool and serve. Thaw prebaked scones in bags at room temperature.

Mix-and-Match Muffins

Home-baked muffins are hard to beat—unless you add more sugar and call them cupcakes.

Packaging: Zip-top freezer bags (gallon size [4 L] for baked muffins, quart size [1 L] for mix)

DRY INGREDIENTS:

3 cups (360 g) unbleached all-purpose flour

½ cup (60 g) whole-wheat flour

4 teaspoons (15 g) baking powder

½ teaspoon baking soda

½ teaspoon salt

1 cup (200 g) granulated or (225 g) light brown sugar

WET INGREDIENTS:

½ cup (120 ml) vegetable oil

1 cup (235 ml) milk

½ cup (112 g) plain yogurt

2 large eggs

Mix-ins: Your choice of 1 teaspoon extract (such as vanilla, almond, butterscotch, or coconut), 1½ cups (225 g) any combination of fruit (such as mashed bananas, finely chopped apples, blueberries, raspberries, or fresh or dried cranberries), chopped nuts, and/or chocolate chips

—
Makes 24 muffins

Preheat the oven to 350°F (180°C or gas mark 4). Line 2 muffin tins with paper liners or spray them with nonstick cooking spray.

In a large bowl, combine the oil, milk, yogurt, and eggs. Whisk to blend. Add the dry ingredients to the wet ingredients and fold gently with a rubber spatula just until combined. Fold in the desired mix-ins.

Scoop the batter into the prepared muffin tins. Bake for 25 to 30 minutes, until the muffins are golden brown and a tester comes out clean. Cool the muffins on a rack.

TO PACKAGE AS A MIX: Place all of the dry ingredients in the quart-size (1 L) freezer bag. Seal the bag and shake it gently to combine the ingredients. Store in the freezer.

FREEZING: Place the cooled muffins in the gallon-size (4 L) freezer bags, removing as much air as possible before sealing the bag. Freeze.

TO THAW AND SERVE: Thaw the muffins in bags at room temperature.

Nutty Zucchini Bread

Ah, zucchini. The vegetable you love to hate, or hate to love. They are such prolific little buggers. When I have a wealth of zucchini from his garden, I bake up a big batch of this bread. A food processor is very handy for this sort of thing, making quick work of grating zucchini. Feel free to stir in chopped nuts or chocolate chips, or both.

Packaging: Plastic wrap, two gallon-size (4 L) zip-top freezer bags

3 cups (705 ml) vegetable oil

9 large eggs, beaten

5 cups (1000 g) sugar

2 tablespoons (30 ml) vanilla extract

9 cups (1080 g) unbleached all-purpose flour

6 cups (720 g) shredded zucchini

1 tablespoon baking soda

¾ teaspoon baking powder

1 tablespoon (18 g) salt

1 tablespoon ground cinnamon

1½ cups (210 g) chopped nuts of your choice, chocolate chips, or a combination

—
Makes four 9 × 5-inch (23 × 12.7 cm) loaves

Preheat the oven to 325°F (170°C or gas mark 3). Spray four 9 × 5-inch (23 × 12.7 cm) loaf pans with nonstick cooking spray.

In a very large bowl, combine the oil, eggs, sugar, and vanilla. Mix well.

Stir in the flour, shredded zucchini, baking soda, baking powder, salt, cinnamon, and nuts. Stir until just mixed.

Pour the batter into the prepared pans and bake for 1 hour or until a tester inserted in the center comes out clean. Transfer to a rack and let cool for 10 minutes, then remove from the pan and place on a rack to cool completely..

FREEZING: Wrap the cooled loaves in plastic wrap. Place two wrapped loaves in each freezer bag and freeze.

TO THAW AND SERVE: Thaw the bread, wrapped, at room temperature for about 1 hour. Slice and serve.

Whole-Grain Cinnamon Rolls

I used to mix up cinnamon rolls every Saturday night so we could enjoy them on Sunday mornings. While we loved the morning ritual, I wasn't crazy about the messy Saturday night kitchen. My friend Amy taught me how to adapt my cinnamon rolls for the freezer. Now we can enjoy cinnamon rolls any day of the week—without the huge mess! I use a bread machine to make the process even easier.

Packaging: Gallon-size (4 L) zip-top freezer bags

DOUGH:

2 cups (470 ml) milk

4½ tablespoons (63 g) unsalted butter

1½ teaspoons vanilla extract

¼ cup (50 g) granulated sugar

3¾ teaspoons active dry yeast

½ cup (40 g) quick-cooking rolled oats

1 cup (120 g) whole-wheat flour

3 to 3½ cups (360 to 420 g) unbleached all-purpose flour

1¾ teaspoons salt

FILLING:

3½ tablespoons (50 g) unsalted butter, softened

¾ cup (150 g) light or dark brown sugar

1 tablespoon ground cinnamon

WHEN READY TO SERVE, YOU WILL NEED:

¾ cup (90 g) confectioners' sugar

1 to 2 tablespoons (15 to 30 ml) milk

½ teaspoon vanilla extract

—
Makes 18 rolls

Line baking sheets with parchment paper.

If making the dough in the bread machine, combine the dough ingredients in the bread machine according to the manufacturer's instructions. Program the machine for the dough setting and start it.

If making the dough by hand, place the milk and butter in a medium saucepan and warm slightly. Transfer the mixture to a large bowl or the bowl of a stand mixer and add the vanilla, sugar, and yeast. Stir and allow the yeast to proof for 5 minutes. Add the oats, whole-wheat flour, 3 cups (360 g) of the all-purpose flour, and the salt. Stir to combine well. Knead in the stand mixer with the dough hook or turn the mixture out onto a lightly floured surface and knead by hand. Continue kneading for 5 minutes to create a smooth, elastic dough, adding more of the all-purpose flour as necessary. Transfer to a greased bowl and turn the dough ball to coat. Let rise until doubled in bulk, about 1 hour.

(continued)

When the dough is ready, roll it out on a lightly floured surface to form a 12 × 15-inch (30.5 × 38 cm) rectangle.

Spread the softened butter over the surface.

In a small bowl, combine the brown sugar and cinnamon. Sprinkle this mixture over the butter.

Roll up the dough, jelly-roll fashion, starting from a long edge and pinching the seam to seal.

Cut the rolled dough into 18 slices, each about ⅔ inch (1.7 cm) wide, and arrange them on the prepared baking sheets 1 to 2 inches (2.5 to 5 cm) apart.

FREEZING: Place the trays in the freezer and freeze the rolls until they are firm. Remove the trays from the freezer and place the rolls on their sides in the freezer bags, in stacks of six. Place the bags in the freezer immediately.

TO THAW AND SERVE: The night before baking, remove as many rolls as desired from the freezer and place them in a greased 9 × 13-inch (23 × 33 cm) baking dish. You may need 2 pans if you bake all 18 rolls at once. Cover the dish with plastic wrap and refrigerate overnight. The rolls will thaw and rise in the refrigerator. In the morning, remove the dish from the refrigerator and let the rolls rest for 20 minutes at room temperature. Preheat the oven to 350°F (180°C or gas mark 4). Bake the rolls for 20 to 30 minutes, or until browned. Remove the pans from the oven and cool on a wire rack. To make the icing, stir together the confectioners' sugar, milk, and vanilla until smooth. Glaze the rolls with the icing before serving.

Garlic-Parmesan Swirl Biscuits

These biscuits take a little extra work, but they look elegant and really dress up the plate. I have found that preparing and freezing them in advance of baking is the best approach.

GARLIC BUTTER:

¼ cup (56 g) (½ stick) unsalted butter, softened

3 cloves garlic, crushed

2 tablespoons freshly grated Parmesan cheese

¼ teaspoon dried parsley flakes

BISCUIT DOUGH:

2 cups (240 g) unbleached all-purpose flour

1 teaspoon salt

1 tablespoon baking powder

⅓ cup (75 g) unsalted butter

¾ cup (180 ml) milk

—
Makes 12 biscuits

Grease a 12-cup muffin tin.

In a small bowl, combine the garlic butter ingredients. Set aside.

In a large bowl, combine the flour, salt, and baking powder. Cut in the ⅓ cup (75 g) butter with a pastry blender or two knives until coarse crumbs are formed. Stir in the milk until combined.

Turn the dough out onto a floured surface. Knead the dough a few times and flatten into a 9 × 12-inch (23 × 30.5 cm) rectangle.

Spread the garlic butter over the surface of the dough. Roll the dough up from the long side and pinch the edges to seal.

Cut the rolled dough into twelve 1-inch (2.5 cm)-wide pieces. Place each spiral in a prepared muffin cup.

About the Author

Jessica Fisher is the creator of two popular blogs, *Life as Mom* and *Good Cheap Eats*; the author of four cookbooks; and a go-to source for fresh and clever ideas about how to live and eat well on a budget. A mother of six, she lives with her husband and family in the San Diego area.

Index